Target
Get back on track 5

Edexcel GCSE (9–1)
Geography B

John Hopkin
Rebecca Kitchen
Lindsay Frost

P Pearson

Published by Pearson Education Limited, 80 Strand, London, WC2R ORL.

www.pearsonschoolsandfecolleges.co.uk

Copies of official specifications for all Pearson qualifications may be found on the website: qualifications.pearson.com

Text and illustrations © Pearson Education Ltd 2018
Typeset and illustrated by QBS Learning
Produced by QBS Learning

The rights of Lindsay Frost, John Hopkin and Rebecca Kitchen to be identified as authors of this work have been asserted by them in accordance with the Copyright, Designs and Patents Act 1988.

First published 2018

21 20 19 18
10 9 8 7 6 5 4 3 2 1

British Library Cataloguing in Publication Data
A catalogue record for this book is available from the British Library

ISBN 978 0 435 18899 3

Copyright notice
All rights reserved. No part of this publication may be reproduced in any form or by any means (including photocopying or storing it in any medium by electronic means and whether or not transiently or incidentally to some other use of this publication) without the written permission of the copyright owner, except in accordance with the provisions of the Copyright, Designs and Patents Act 1988 or under the terms of a licence issued by the Copyright Licensing Agency, Barnard's Inn, 86 Fetter Lane, London EC4A 1EN (www.cla.co.uk). Applications for the copyright owner's written permission should be addressed to the publisher.

Printed in Slovakia by Neografia

Acknowledgements
The authors and publisher would like to thank the following individuals and organisations for their kind permission to reproduce copyright material.

Maps
Pages 09, 10, 11, 13, 15, 70: © Crown copyright 2017, OS 100030901.

Figures
Page 65: Reproduced with permission from BP p.l.c.

Photographs
(Key: b-bottom; c-centre; l-left; r-right; t-top)
Alamy Stock Photo: Ashley Cooper pics 66l, Oliver Förstner 68; Shutterstock: Albert Pego 66r
All other images © Pearson Education

Note from the publisher
Pearson has robust editorial processes, including answer and fact checks, to ensure the accuracy of the content in this publication, and every effort is made to ensure this publication is free of errors. We are, however, only human, and occasionally errors do occur. Pearson is not liable for any misunderstandings that arise as a result of errors in this publication, but it is our priority to ensure that the content is accurate. If you spot an error, please do contact us at resourcescorrections@pearson.com so we can make sure it is corrected.

Contents

① Tackling thematic map questions

This unit will help you learn how to work with and interpret different types of **thematic** map. The skills you will build are to:

- describe simple patterns or distributions on a map
- improve the way you describe distributions on a map
- find evidence from choropleth maps.

In the exam, you will come across many maps showing features, patterns and distributions. Sometimes you will be asked to practise your geographical skills directly with a map – for example, by identifying features or finding data. Often you will also have to interpret a map – for example, by describing what it shows.

Exam-style question

Study **Figure 1**, which shows patterns of inequality in Birmingham, UK.

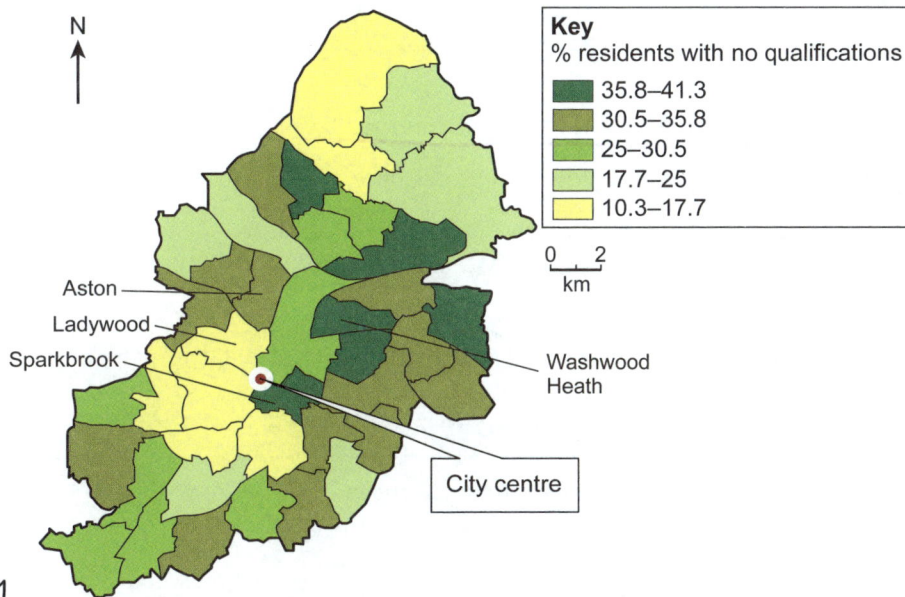

Key
% residents with no qualifications

- 35.8–41.3
- 30.5–35.8
- 25–30.5
- 17.7–25
- 10.3–17.7

0   2 km

Aston
Ladywood
Sparkbrook
Washwood Heath
City centre

Figure 1

i   Name **one** ward with 35.8–41.3% of residents with no qualifications.   *sparkbrook*   (1 mark)

ii   Describe the distribution of residents with no qualifications in Birmingham.   (3 marks)
there is less people with no qualifications and people with no qualifications on the outside.

The three key questions in the **skills boosts** will help you to develop your map skills before you prepare your own response to the exam-style question above.

| 1 | **How do I describe patterns or distributions on a map?** | 2 | **How can I improve my descriptions of maps?** | 3 | **How do I interpret choropleth maps?** |

Before you can answer any map questions, you need to check you understand **the map** and **the question**. Look at this exam-style question.

Exam-style question

Study **Figure 2**, which shows the world's largest megacities in 2014.

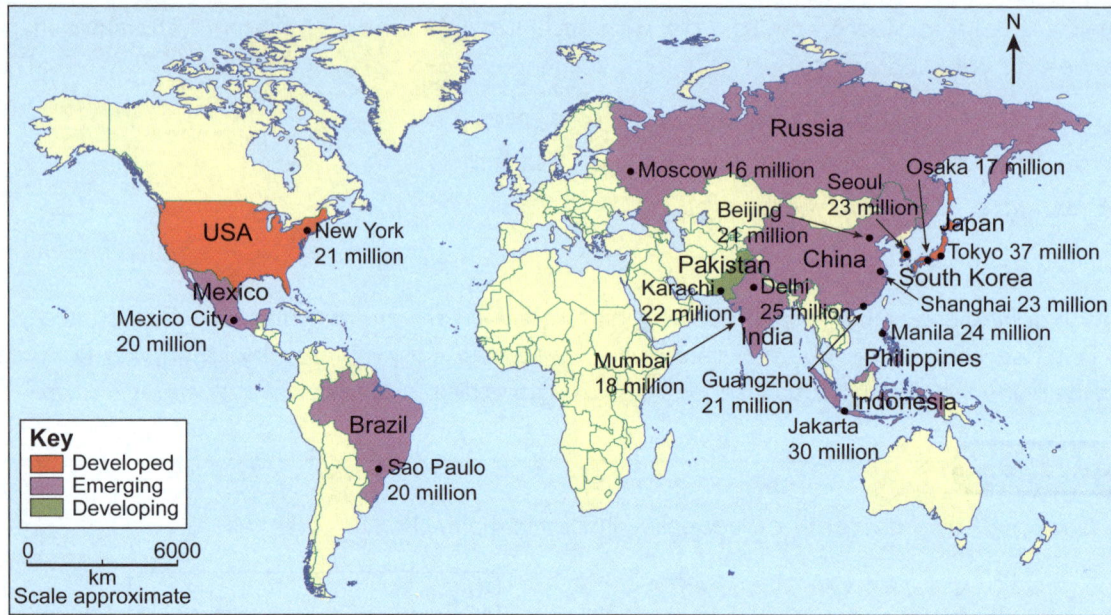

Figure 2

i State the population of the world's largest megacity. (1 mark)
Tokyo

ii Name **one** large megacity in a developing country. (1 mark)
Karachi

iii Describe the global distribution of the largest megacities. (2 marks)
Most are in the North east or south west

① What exactly is **the map** about? Write ✏ short notes about the map below.

Title: What is the map about?	*Showing worlds largest megacities in 2014*
Key: In more detail, what does the map show?	*The shading shows Developed, Emerging and Developing megacities.*
Scale: How big is it?	*The scale is 1 cm = 3000 km*
Direction: Which way is north?	*towards the top of the map.*

② What exactly is **the question** asking me to do? Highlight ✏ the command words.

> The **command word** is a verb which tells you what to do in your answer. Always underline or highlight the command word, as well as any other important words that help you organise your response.

③ Now write ✏ the answers to exam-style question parts i and ii below.

i ....

ii ....

1 How do I describe patterns or distributions on maps?

You will often be asked to 'describe' patterns, distributions or features in geography. Before you can write a good description, you need to check you understand the meaning of the command word '**describe**' and how to use the marks to guide your response.

Look at exam-style question part iii and **Figure 2** on page 2. It is a 'describe' question.

Here you need to focus on the global distribution of large megacities.

Describe: Give an account of the main characteristics of something or the steps in a process. Statements in the response should be developed but do not need to include a justification or reason.

For 2 marks, you need to make **two** good points, which are expanded to show your knowledge.

Do not explain or give reasons – you won't get marks for doing so.

1 Now look at how two students responded to the question. In Yasmin's first statement, her point and development are highlighted.

Yasmin

> Figure 2 shows the majority of the world's largest megacities are in emerging countries, especially in Asian countries like China. There are only three developed countries with large megacities – they are USA, South Korea and Japan. Pakistan is the only developing country with a megacity, Karachi, with 22 million people.

/2

Sam

> Most of the world's megacities are in emerging countries such as China. Tokyo, Japan, is the largest megacity with an amazing 37 million people.

/2

a Use colour-coding to highlight ✐ any further points and developments the students have made.

b How effective is each student's answer? Rate them out of 2 ✐. Note ✐ down one way each student could improve their response.

Yasmin: ....

....

....

Sam: ....

....

....

2 Now write ✐ one more statement including a point and development.

....

....

....

2 How can I improve my descriptions of maps?

An easy mistake to make when describing a distribution is to give reasons or explanations for it. Avoid this by using the **Pattern–Qualification–Exception (PQE)** rule.

You have learned to write simple but effective descriptions using Point – Develop. Sometimes you can improve your description of distributions on a map by using **PQE** to add detail.

P = general pattern or distribution

Q = qualifications or additional details

E = exceptions to the pattern or distribution

Now look at this exam-style question and Kate's response below.

Exam-style question

ii Describe the distribution of hurricanes.   (3 marks)

Key
- Areas with tropical storms
- → Hurricanes
- → Cyclones
- → Typhoons

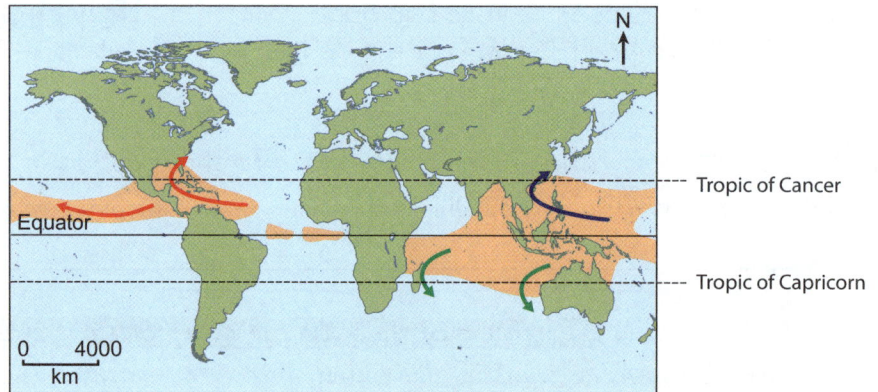

Equator

Tropic of Cancer

Tropic of Capricorn

N

0   4000
km

Figure 3

The map shows that hurricanes form in the Atlantic and Pacific Oceans close to the Equator, because they need warm water to form. For example, many hurricanes start out in the Atlantic Ocean and travel westwards towards the Caribbean and Central America. Hurricanes are a hazard mainly affecting places between the Tropics of Cancer and Capricorn, but some reach the eastern parts of the USA.

(1) Use colour-coding to highlight 🖊 Kate's use of PQE.

(2) Underline Ⓐ all the geographical words that support the description.

(3) Find **one** phrase or sentence that Kate did not need to include. Circle Ⓐ it. Write 🖊 a sentence explaining your choice.

> Good descriptions include some geography! Notice how Kate uses geographical language about places to link her response to the question.

(4) Now look at this exam-style question.

Write 🖊 your response on paper. Use colour-coding to highlight 🖊 your use of PQE.

Exam-style question

ii Describe the global distribution of cyclones.   (3 marks)

3   How do I interpret choropleth maps?

Choropleth maps are common in the geography exam. When you are working with choropleth maps, you must make sure you are clear about what the key tells you.

Look closely at the key to **Figure 4** in this exam-style question. It shows the population density, or the number of people per square kilometre.

Exam-style question

i   Describe the population density of the British Isles south and east of the line from the River Tees to the River Exe.   **(2 marks)**

ii Describe the population density of the British Isles north and west of the line from the River Tees to the River Exe.   **(2 marks)**

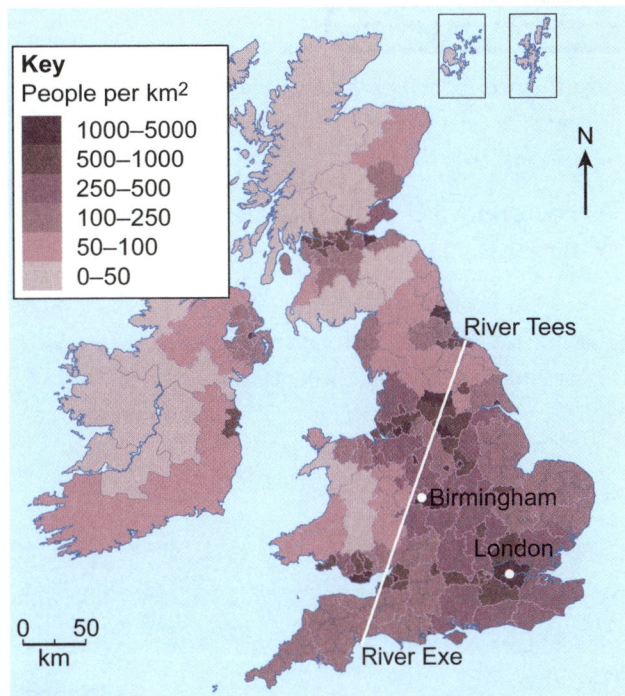

Choropleth maps are shaded to show areas with high, medium and low values. In this map, you should be able to find:
- high population density (dark shading)
- medium population density (medium shading)
- low population density (light shading).

Key
People per km²
- 1000–5000
- 500–1000
- 250–500
- 100–250
- 50–100
- 0–50

N

River Tees

Birmingham

London

0   50
km

River Exe

Figure 4

1   Draft ✎ a response to exam-style question part i on paper, using **Point – Develop** to help structure your writing. Make **two** points and develop both. Follow the example below.

Point	Develop
South and east of the Tees-Exe line, the population density is...	For example,...

2   Now draft ✎ a response to exam-style question part ii on paper using PQE. Make **two** points and follow the example below.

Pattern	Qualification	Exception
The population density in this half of the British Isles is ...	In particular, much of Scotland ...	However, there are exceptions. For example, ...

Sample response

To do well with map questions, you should:

- check the map, including the title, key, scale and direction
- use the command word(s) and mark(s) to guide your response
- structure your writing to make sure you develop each point when describing distributions.

Look at this exam-style question.

Exam-style question

Study **Figure 5**, which shows patterns of inequality and benefit claimants in Birmingham, UK.

i   Name **one** ward with 336–560 benefit claimants.

(1 mark)

ii Describe the pattern of residents claiming benefits in Birmingham.

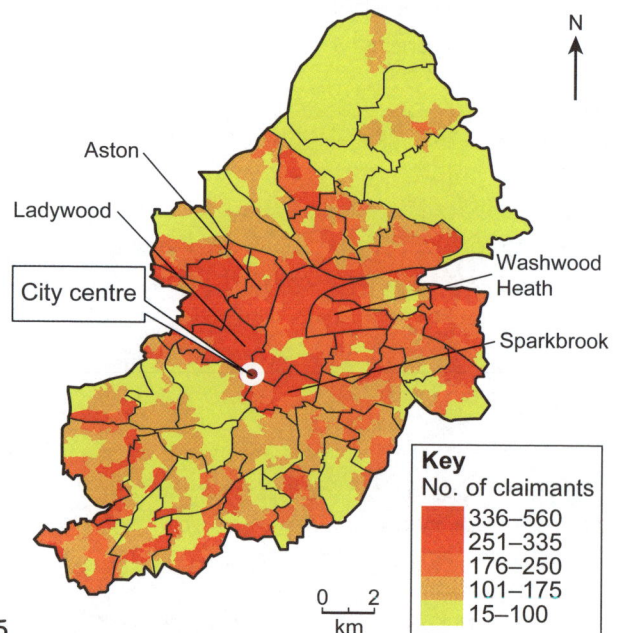

(3 marks)

Figure 5

Aston
Ladywood
City centre
Washwood Heath
Sparkbrook

Key
No. of claimants
336–560
251–335
176–250
101–175
15–100

0   2
km

N

(1) Look at the students' responses to the exam-style question part ii.

Yasmin

In Birmingham, inner city wards like Washwood Heath, Aston, Ladywood and Sparkbrook have most benefit claimants as shown on the key. Away from the city centre, in the suburbs towards the top of the map, there are many less claimants. These areas are shaded yellow.

Sam

Overall, the inner-city wards have the highest number of claimants. For example Ladypool and Aston both have 336–500 claimants. Further away from the centre, most wards have fewer claimants, especially in the north of Birmingham where nearly everywhere has 15–100 claimants. There are some exceptions. There are higher numbers of benefit claimants on the south edge of the city and right in the city centre where fewer people...

a   Which student used **Point – Develop** and which used **Pattern – Qualification – Exception**? Write ✏ PD or PQE beside the student's name.

b   Underline Ⓐ the best points in each response.

c   Write ✏ a sentence or two on paper, giving feedback on each response.

Your turn!

You are now going to write your response to this exam-style question.

Exam-style question

Study **Figure 1** on page 1, which shows patterns of inequality in Birmingham, UK.

i Name **one** ward with 35.8–41.3% of residents with no qualifications. (1 mark)

ii Describe the distribution of residents with no qualifications in Birmingham. (3 marks)

1 Write 🖊 your response to part i. ....

Now look at part ii. Think about what you have covered in this unit.

2 Practise the checks you worked through on page 2. This time, run through the checks in your head. Then underline Ⓐ the important words in the question and circle Ⓐ the important features on the map.

3 Now write 🖊 your response to part ii, using **Point** – **Development** to structure your writing.

Point	Develop

4 Try to improve your description. Rewrite 🖊 your response, using **PQE** to structure your writing.

Pattern	Qualification	Exception

Review your skills

Check up

Review your response to the exam-style question on page 7. Tick ✓ the column to show how well you think you have done each of the following.

	Not quite ✓	Nearly there ✓	Got it! ✓
checked the map and followed the question and command word	☐	☐	☐
structured a description of a map using point – develop	☐	☐	☐
structured a description of a map using pattern – qualification – exception	☐	☐	☐
interpreted a choropleth map accurately	☐	☐	☐

Look over all of your work in this unit. Note ✏ down the **three** most important things you need to remember when working with thematic maps showing distributions in geography.

① ....

② ....

③ ....

Need more practice?

Look again at **Figure 2** on page 2, which shows the world's largest megacities in 2014. Use **PQE** to improve on your description of the distribution of the largest megacities (page 3). This time, write ✏ a description aiming for **3 marks**.

How confident do you feel about each of these **skills**? Colour ✏ in the bars.

1 How do I describe patterns or distributions on a map?

2 How can I improve my descriptions of maps?

3 How do I interpret choropleth maps?

② Developing OS map skills

This unit will help you learn how to identify features on 1:25,000 and 1:50,000 scale Ordnance Survey (OS) maps, and interpret the maps by describing the landscape. The skills you will build are to:

- use scale and find distances on OS maps
- use four- and six-figure grid references to locate places on maps
- use contour patterns to understand landscapes.

In the exam, you can be asked to tackle 1:25,000 and/or 1:50,000 OS map questions in any of the three papers. This unit will prepare you to respond to exam questions based on OS maps like the one below, or maps of urban landscapes like the one on page 10.

Exam-style question

Study **Figure 1**, which is a 1:50,000 scale Ordnance Survey extract showing Swanage Bay, Dorset.

i   Identify the landform in grid square 0281.   (1 mark)

☒ A Valley with gentle slopes

☒ B Valley with steep slopes

☒ C Ridge with steep slopes

☒ D Area of flat land

ii   State the straight-line distance between Ballard Point at 048813 and the caravan site at 024808.   (1 mark)

iii Suggest **two** reasons for the sea defences in grid square 0379.   (4 marks)

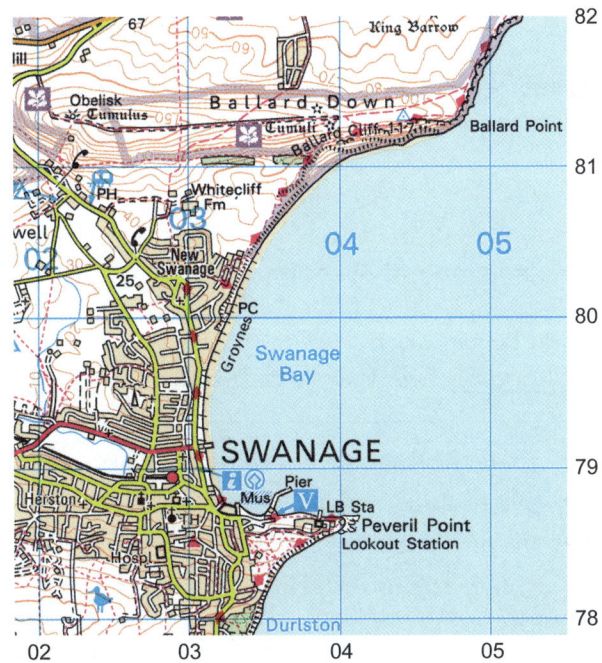

Figure 1

© Crown copyright 2016 OS 100030901

Remember: North is always at the top of an OS map, and south is at the bottom. So east is to the right, and west is to the left.

The three key questions in the **skills boosts** will help you develop your skills before you prepare your own response to this OS map question.

① **How do I use scale and find distances on OS maps?**

② **How do I use grid references?**

③ **How do I use contour patterns to understand landscapes?**

© Crown copyright 2016 OS 100030901

Exam-style question

Study **Figure 2**, which is a 1:50,000 scale Ordnance Survey extract showing part of the River Dee and Chester.

i   Identify the main land use in grid square 3866. **(1 mark)**

ii State the distance, by road, between Bank Farm at 375672 and Higher Ferry House at 370659. **(1 mark)**

iii Suggest **two** reasons why the land north of the River Dee is at risk of flooding. **(4 marks)**

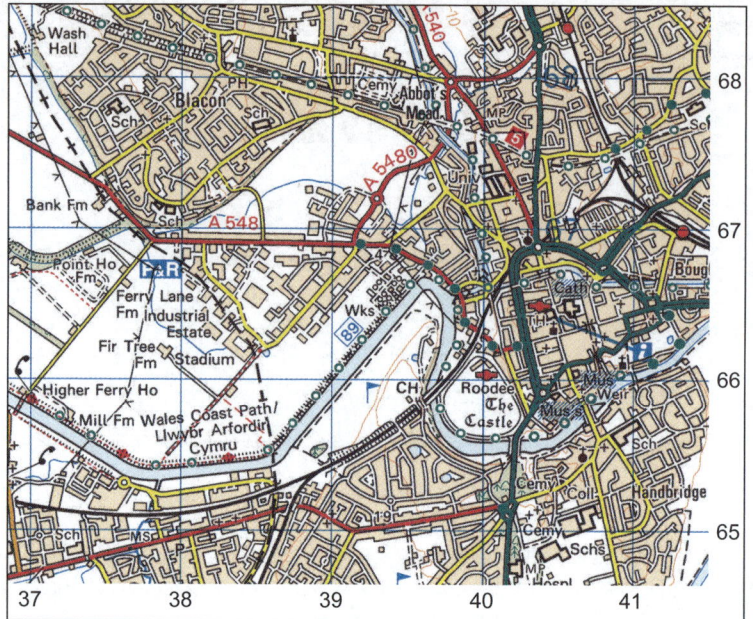

Figure 2

Suggest: Apply understanding to provide a reasoned explanation of how or why something may occur. A suggested explanation requires a justification/exemplification of a point.

Give short explanation/s, not descriptions.

Use **Point – Develop** to make sure of the marks.

Part iii is a 'suggest' question.

① Jade began work on part iii. She spotted a key phrase in the question and underlined it: is at risk of flooding. She then jotted down some notes.

- Industrial estate – factories at risk
- No contours – flat land
- Flood defences or embankment along river
- Small streams nearby

Use evidence from the map to add 🖊 to Jade's notes.

② Jade then used her notes to start writing a response to part iii. Notice how she uses the conjunction 'so' to link together her point and development.

This land is at risk of flooding as it is flat, with no contours, so floodwater could move quickly across a large area. ....

a   Write 🖊 **two** more sentences responding to part iii.

b   Use colour-coding to highlight 🖊 your points, developments and conjunctions.

....

....

10   **Unit 2 Developing OS map skills**

① How do I use scale and find distances on OS maps?

When you are working with 1:25,000 and 1:50,000 scale OS maps, getting the scales right is vital if you want to calculate distances.

Look at the difference between the two maps.

- 1:50,000 OS maps (**Figure 2** on page 10) have grid squares that measure 2 cm across. This represents 1 km in real life.

- 1:25,000 OS maps (**Figure 3**) have grid squares measuring 4 cm across. This also represents 1 km in real life.

① Study **Figure 2** on page 10 and **Figure 3** here. Use a ruler to measure 🖉 the grid squares on each map.

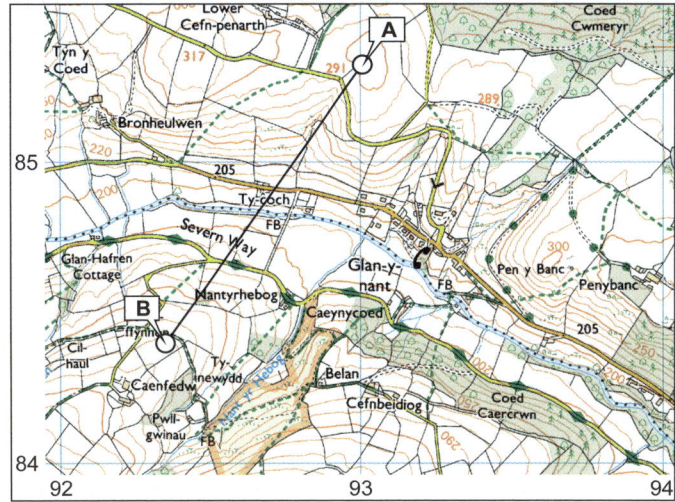

© Crown copyright 2016 OS 100030901

Figure 3 A 1:25,000 scale OS extract of the River Severn, Powys

On a 1:25,000 map, the scale is a ratio of 4 cm = 1 km. Jade used a ruler to measure the distance between places **W** and **X** and found they were 10 cm apart.

Using the ratio, she calculated the distance between **W** and **X**:

$$\frac{10}{4} \text{ cm} = 2.5 \text{ km in real life}$$

② Jade measured the distance between places **Y** and **Z** on the same map. It was 13 cm. Calculate 🖉 the distance between **Y** and **Z** in real life.

Distance between **Y** and **Z**: ....

③ Study **Figure 3** above.

  a Measure the distance between places **A** and **B**. Note 🖉 it down. ....

  b Calculate 🖉 the distance in real life. ....

  ....

④ Study **Figure 2** on page 10. On a 1:50,000 map the scale is a ratio of 2 cm = 1 km.

  a Measure the distance between Wash Hall (north-west corner of the map) and the Castle (by the river). Write 🖉 it down. ....

  b Calculate 🖉 the distance in real life. ....

  ....

2 How do I use grid references?

OS maps are divided into numbered grid squares. The numbers across the top and bottom of the map are called **eastings**. The numbers up the sides are called **northings**. When locating places on a map, make sure you use the eastings first, and then the northings.

Four-figure grid references are used to find the wider location of features.

Look at **Figure 4** to see how to find the grid square 3866.

Remember: Go along the corridor and then up the stairs.

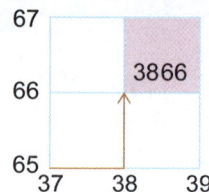

Figure 4 Finding the wider location

① Look again at **Figure 2** on page 10. David identified some features using four-figure grid references, but made some mistakes.

		✓ or ✗	Correction
The golf course south of the River Dee	3965		
Chester city centre, around the cathedral	6640		
The suburb of Handbridge south of the city centre	4065		

   a Tick ✓ David's correct answers and cross ✗ the incorrect ones.

   b Write ✎ the correct answers in the last column of the table.

   c Annotate ✎ the table, explaining where David went wrong.

Six-figure grid references are used to pinpoint the exact location of features.

In **Figure 5**, the original 3866 square is divided into 100 imaginary squares (10 horizontally by 10 vertically).

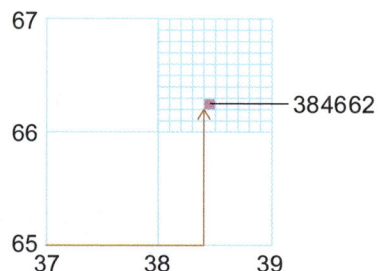

The exact location of the Stadium in the pink square is 384 662.

Figure 5 Pinpointing the exact location

② Look again at **Figure 2** on page 10. David identified some features using six-figure grid references, but made some mistakes.

		✓ or ✗	Correction
Chester railway station	415670		
Chester cathedral	406665		
The Club House on Chester golf course	393659		

   a Tick ✓ David's correct answers and cross ✗ the incorrect ones.

   b Write ✎ the correct answers in the last column of the table.

   c Annotate ✎ the table, explaining where David went wrong.

3 **How do I use contour patterns to understand landscapes?**

Contours are lines joining places of equal height above sea level. They also tell us about how much the land slopes, and where there are hills and valleys. A **spot height** is a dot on the map with the exact height of the land in metres.

Contours are 5 metres apart on 1:25,000 maps, and 10 metres apart on 1:50,000 maps.

Use **Figure 6** to work out the shape of the land.

- Contours close together show the land slopes steeply.
- Contours far apart show a gentle slope.
- Few contours or no contours show the land is flat.
- A valley is where contours form a V-shape, with higher land on each side.
- A ridge is where contours are in a V-shape, with lower land on each side.
- Hills have contours going around them on four sides.

Look carefully at the contour heights so you don't get valleys, hills and ridges muddled up.

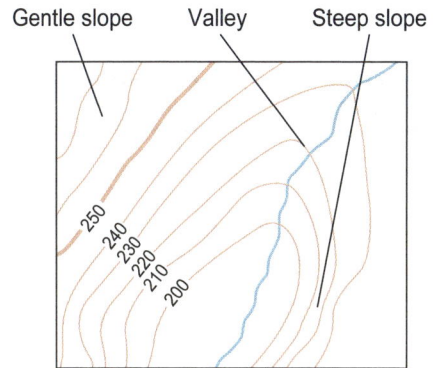

Figure 6 Contour patterns

1 Look at **Figure 7** below.

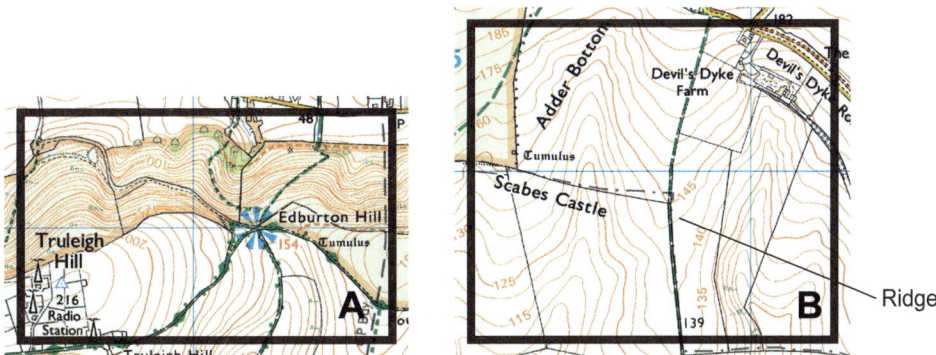

Figure 7 1:25,000 OS map extracts of the South Downs

© Crown copyright 2016 OS 100030901

a Which of the following best describes the landscape shown by the contour patterns in area **A**? Tick it. ✓

i Mostly flat with some gentle slopes ☐

ii Very steeply sloping ☐

iii Both steep and very steep slopes ☐

iv Gently sloping ☐

First, put a line through two options that are obviously wrong. Then choose the best option remaining.

b i Find and circle Ⓐ the 139 metre spot height in area **B**.

ii Find and circle Ⓐ **one** other spot height on the map extracts.

c Label on the maps ✏ **two** examples of:

i a hill

ii a valley

iii a ridge (one has been labelled for you).

Sample response

To do well with OS map questions, you should:

- check the scale of the map and use it to calculate distances
- go along the corridor and up the stairs when using four- and six-figure grid references
- use contour patterns to help identify the shape of the land.

Now look at this exam-style question and **Figure 2** on page 10.

Now look at this exam-style question and **Figure 2** on page 10.

Exam-style question

i	Identify the main land use in grid square 3866.	(1 mark)
ii	State the distance, by road, between Bank Farm at 375672 and Higher Ferry House at 370659.	(1 mark)
iii	Suggest **two** reasons why the land north of the River Dee is at risk of flooding.	(4 marks)

1 Look at Jade's and Abid's responses to parts i and ii.

Jade

i	Industrial estate	☐
ii	1.4 km	☐
Feedback		

Abid

i	Farmland	☐
ii	1.75 km	☐
Feedback		

a Check **Figure 2** on page 10 to find out which of the students' answers are correct. Mark them with a tick ✓ or a cross ✗.

b Focus on the wrong answers. Look back at Skills boosts 1 and 2, then write ✎ feedback to help correct their mistakes.

2 Now look at Abid's response to part iii below.

> There is an embankment in 3865 so flooding is obviously a risk nearby. The land here has no contours – it is flat and at risk of flooding and as a result floodwater could move quickly across a large area, causing damage. There are also a number of small streams in the area and nearby farmland.

a Use colour-coding to highlight ✎ Abid's points, development and any conjunctions he used.

b Strike through ~~cat~~ any parts that don't work well.

c How effective is Abid's response? Write ✎ a sentence or two giving feedback.

....

....

Your turn!

You are now going to write your response to this exam-style question.

© Crown copyright 2016 OS 100030901

Exam-style question

Study **Figure 1**, which is a 1:50,000 scale Ordnance Survey extract showing Swanage Bay, Dorset.

i   Identify the landform in grid square 0281.   **(1 mark)**

   ☒ A   Valley with gentle slopes

   ☒ B   Valley with steep slopes

   ☒ C   Ridge with steep slopes

   ☒ D   Area of flat land

ii   State the straight-line distance between Ballard Point at 048813 and the caravan site at 024808.   **(1 mark)**

iii   Suggest **two** reasons for the sea defences in grid square 0379.   **(4 marks)**

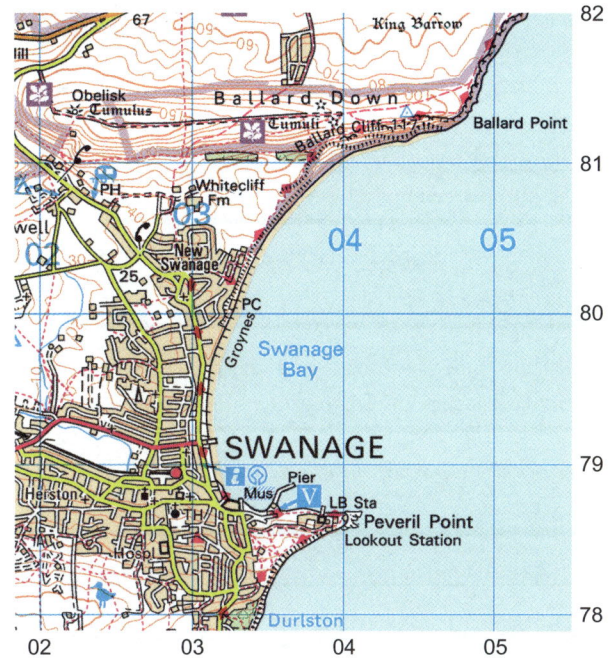

Figure 1

① Which landform is in grid square 0281? Cross ⊗ your response in part i above.

② Write ✎ your response to part ii here. .... km

③ Look at part iii. Underline Ⓐ any key phrases in the question. Then quickly jot ✎ down some notes in the space below.

④ Now write ✎ your response to part iii on paper, using **Point** – **Development** to structure your writing. Use the box below to help you plan your response. You could choose some conjunctions from the bank on the right to help you link them.

Conjunctions bank	
because	so
as a result	for this reason

Point	Develop

Review your skills

Check up

Review your response to the exam-style question on page 15. Tick ✓ the column to show how well you think you have done each of the following.

	Not quite ✓	Nearly there ✓	Got it! ✓
checked the map and followed the question and command word	☐	☐	☐
used scale to measure and calculate distances accurately	☐	☐	☐
used four- and six-figure grid references to locate places on OS maps	☐	☐	☐
used contour patterns to understand landscapes	☐	☐	☐

Need more practice?

Tackle this task to revise your OS map skills. Draw ✎ a line linking the skills to an appropriate tip to help you remember them.

Skill	Tip
contour lines	along the corridor and up the stairs
direction	far apart for gentle slopes, close together for steep slopes
distance	a dot on the map with the height of the land in metres
grid references	always 1 km square
grid squares	1:25,000: 4 cm = 1 km / 1:50,000: 2 cm = 1 km
spot height	north is always at the top of the map

How confident do you feel about each of these **skills**? Colour ✎ in the bars.

① **How do I use scale and find distances on OS maps?**
▭ ▭ ▭ ▭

② **How do I use grid references?**
▭ ▭ ▭ ▭

③ **How do I use contour patterns to understand landscapes?**
▭ ▭ ▭ ▭

3 Working with photographs and questions about processes

This unit will help you learn how to work with photographs and write good descriptions and explanations of the physical and human processes in geography. The skills you will build are to:

- write an effective description of geographical processes
- improve your use of geographical language
- write an effective explanation of geographical processes.

Processes are the physical and/or human actions that change places and environments. Processes happen in stages, and have causes and effects. For example, how a landform is created.

In the exam, you will be asked to tackle questions that require you to find evidence from photographs such as the one below. You will also be asked to describe or explain processes in physical and human geography. This unit will prepare you to write your own response to this question.

Exam-style question

Study **Figure 1**, which shows a landscape on the south Devon coast.

i   Which landform is shown at X?   **(1 mark)**

☒ A   a spit

☒ B   an estuary

☒ C   a lagoon

☒ D   saltmarsh

ii   Landform Y is a bar. Explain how a bar is formed.   **(4 marks)**

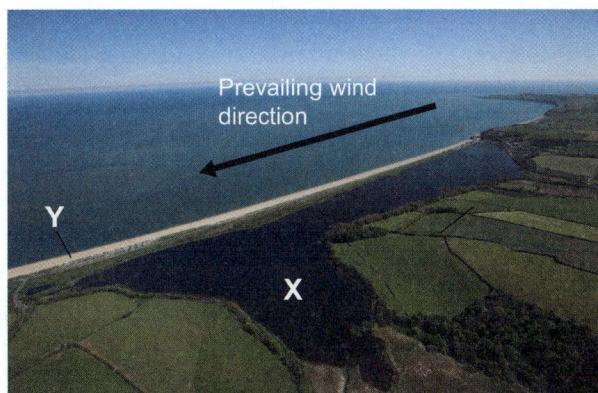

Figure 1

The three key questions in the **skills boosts** will help you to prepare your response.

1. How do I write a good description of geographical processes?

2. How can I improve my use of geographical language?

3. How do I write a good explanation of geographical processes?

In the exam, photographs are often used to show geographical landscapes and features. Use clues in the question and scan the photograph to look for evidence to help you show your understanding of geographical processes. Look at this exam-style question.

Exam-style question

Study **Figure 2**, which shows part of the valley of the River Severn in Shropshire.

i   Identify feature X.   **(1 mark)**

☒   A   a slip-off slope

☒   B   a river cliff

☒   C   a meander

☒   D   an oxbow lake

ii   Landform Y is a meander. Explain how a meander is formed.   **(4 marks)**

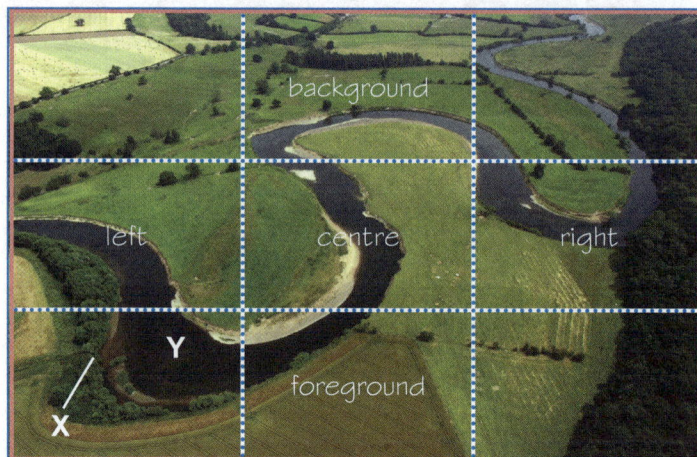

Figure 2

What exactly does **the photograph** show?

One way to approach this is to think about the different parts of a photograph: the foreground and background, centre, and left and right sides.

1   Two students talked about the landscape in **Figure 2** and noted down their observations.

Features	several small fields	sloping valley sides	meandering river	flat flood plain	wooded slope
Part of Figure 2	background				

Can you identify which parts of the photograph they are talking about? Complete 🖉 the students' notes showing where in the photograph the features are. One has been done for you.

2   The students identified feature X as a river cliff.

a   Are they correct? Mark with a tick ✓ if you agree or a cross ✗ if you don't. ☐

b   Write 🖉 a sentence or two explaining your choice.

....

....

c   Can you identify any other features? Add 🖉 labels to **Figure 2** to show where these features are.

> Labels identify what a feature is. Draw a straight, ruled line from the label to the feature.

1 How do I write a good description of geographical processes?

You have already looked at how to **describe** patterns and distributions in Unit 1. Here, you will focus on writing good descriptions of geographical processes.

Look again at **Figure 2** on page 18. Landform Y is a meander. How would you describe the process in the formation of a meander? First, remind yourself of the definition of 'describe'.

Here, you need to focus on the stages in how a meander forms.

Describe: Give an account of the main characteristics of something or the steps in a process. Statements in the response should be developed but do not need to include a justification or reason.

Use Point – Develop to show your knowledge.

The 'ingredients' for a good description of a process:

- start with a short statement to help you focus
- include well-developed points
- use conjunctions to set out a sequence of events/processes in the correct order
- use geographical language – for example, about landforms and processes.

Mary studied **Figure 2** on page 18 and made some notes about how a meander forms.

• bend	• lateral erosion	• slip-off slope	• undercutting	• deposition
• high velocity	• river cliff	• outside/inside bend	• meander neck	• flood plain

She began her response, using sequencing conjunctions to help her describe the process.

Read Mary's response below.

Sequencing conjunctions		
firstly/secondly	to begin with	next/then
in addition	subsequently	finally

I'll describe how a meander forms. Firstly, wide bends form where the river valley is wider and flatter, like the Severn valley in Shropshire in Figure 2. Secondly, lateral erosion happens on the outside of a bend...

1. Highlight ✏ any conjunctions and underline Ⓐ any geographical language Mary uses. Use the conjunctions in the word box to help you.

2. Write ✏ the rest of Mary's description on paper. Use her notes and the sequencing conjunctions to help you add structure and detail. Rewrite Mary's points if you can improve on them.

3. Look again at **Figure 2** on page 18 and the ingredients for a good description above. Then work with a partner to review how effective your final description is.

2 **How can I improve my use of geographical language?**

One way to show your knowledge and understanding of geographical processes is by using geographical language – that is, the vocabulary you choose to identify and describe places, features and processes.

Look at three types of geographical vocabulary below.

Names of places or features – for example, **River Severn**. Using a name will help you to focus on examples you can identify or remember.

Terms for geographical features – for example, **lagoon**. There is often an alternative, everyday word for these features, such as 'lake', but using the geographical term is more accurate.

Terms for geographical processes – for example, **longshore drift**. Using precise terms correctly will help you to demonstrate your understanding of the processes.

Many of these terms are proper nouns, nouns or noun phrases. Adjectives, like *deep*, *wide* or *rapidly*, can also be useful, especially for writing descriptions.

Nathan

The River Severn winds lazily through fertile farmland in its broad, verdant valley. Its sinuous bends (or meanders) are the result of complex geographical processes which leave sediments on the flat land each side of the river.

Amandeep

course

Meanders like those on the River Severn form in the middle and lower part of a river where the valley is wide and flat. The river wears away at the outside of bends, where the water is faster. It forms steeper banks and the bends get larger and closer to each other. Eventually, only a small piece of land separates these twisty bends which are called meanders.

① Read Amandeep's and Nathan's descriptions about how meanders form.

a Use colour-coding to highlight 🖉 the nouns they use for places, geographical features and processes.

b Label 🖉 where they use everyday words, but a geographical term would improve their writing. One has been done for you.

c Circle Ⓐ any adjectives they use to help their descriptions.

② Write 🖉 down what Nathan should do to improve his geographical response.

....

....

....

③ Paper 2 in the exam is worth 94 marks. You will have 1 hour and 30 minutes to complete it. How many minutes do you think you should spend on a question worth 3 marks? Tick ✓ your answer.

2 minutes ☐   3 minutes ☐   6 minutes ☐   9 minutes ☐

3 How do I write a good explanation of geographical processes?

'Explain' questions are very common in the geography exam. Before you can write a good explanation, you need to check you understand the meaning of the command word 'explain'.

Look at this exam-style question and **Figure 1** on page 17. This is an explain question.

Exam-style question

ii Landform Y is a bar. Explain how a bar is formed. (4 marks)

Focus on reasons and explanations, **not** descriptions.

Explain: Provide a reasoned explanation of how or why something occurs. An explanation requires a justification/exemplification of a point. Some questions will require the use of annotated diagrams to support explanation.

For this question, you need to make **four** points about bars, each developed with a reason or an example.

The 'ingredients' for good explanations of a process:

- start with a short statement to help you focus
- have the same number of points as marks; each point gives a reason or an example
- use conjunctions to explain **why** the process happens
- include geographical language – for example, about landforms and processes
- focus on explaining, **not** describing.

You can use cause/effect conjunctions to improve your explanations.

Look at Nathan's explanation below.

Cause/effect conjunctions				
as a result	because	due to	so	therefore
for this reason	thus	since	as	consequently

The formation of a bar results from a process that moves sediment along the coast. This starts with the wind causing the swash to move the sediment up the beach at an angle. Due to gravity, the backwash brings the wave down the beach. This transports the beach sediment along the coast, consequently when it comes to the mouth of a bay, this forms a spit which sticks out from the coast.

1 Highlight ✏ any cause/effect conjunctions and underline Ⓐ any geographical language Nathan uses.

2 Note ✏ down on paper **two** things you think would improve his explanation of how a bar forms.

Sample response

To write a clear response to an 'explain' question based on a photograph, you should:

- study all parts of the photograph for evidence to use in your response
- include the ingredients that make up a good explanation – reasoned points or examples, geographical language and conjunctions
- make sure you give reasons and explain, not simply describe the process.

Look again at the exam-style question and the ingredients for a good explanation on page 21. Then read Amandeep's response below.

Amandeep

> I am going to describe how the bar in Figure 1 was formed. A long time ago longshore drift moved sediments like sand and pebbles along the coastline away from the prevailing wind. Then at a bay or river mouth, the transported material was deposited offshore. Next a spit forms, stretching across the bay. When the spit reaches land on the far side of the bay, a lagoon forms because streams can't reach the sea.

1 Highlight 🖉 two or three good points in Amandeep's explanation. Underline Ⓐ one weakness or mistake in her writing.

2 Amandeep's explanation is not complete. Note 🖉 down **two** things you think would improve her explanation of how a bar forms.

   i ....

   ....

   ii ....

   ....

3 Discuss Amandeep's response with a friend.

   a How effective is her answer? Rate it out of 4 🖉.

   b Make notes 🖉 in the table below explaining how well she met the criteria for writing a clear response to an 'explain' question.

	Amandeep	/4
Uses the photograph, caption, command word and mark to guide her response		
Includes the ingredients for a good explanation		
Focuses on explaining, not describing		

Your turn!

You are now going to write your response to this exam-style question.

Exam-style question

Study **Figure 1**, which shows a landscape on the south Devon coast.

i   Which landform is shown at X?   **(1 mark)**

   ⊠ A   a spit

   ⊠ B   an estuary

   ⊠ C   a lagoon

   ⊠ D   saltmarsh

ii   Landform Y is a bar. Explain how a bar is formed.   **(4 marks)**

Prevailing wind direction

Y

X

Figure 1

(1) Work through and give your answers to the exam-style questions here.

i   Put a cross ⊗ in the box to show the landform.

ii   Look again at the ingredients and student response on page 21. Then write ✏ your own response to part ii in the space below. You could time yourself.

> An opening statement could be part of your first developed point.

Opening statement or phrase	
Point 1	
Point 2	
Point 3	
Point 4	

(2) Now highlight or add callouts ✏ to your response to question **ii** to show how you have written a good explanation. Look again at the ingredients if you are not sure.

(3) Write ✏ down any ways you could improve your explanation. For example, are all your points fully developed?

....

....

....

Review your skills

Check up

Review your response to the exam-style question on page 23. Tick ✓ the column to show how well you think you have done each of the following.

	Not quite ✓	Nearly there ✓	Got it! ✓
studied all parts of the photograph for evidence to use in your response	☐	☐	☐
used effective geographical language and conjunctions effectively	☐	☐	☐
included the ingredients for a good explanation	☐	☐	☐

Look over all your work in this unit. Note ✐ down the **three** most important things you need to remember working with photographs in the exam, and writing descriptions and explanations about processes in geography.

① ....

② ....

③ ....

Need more practice?

Plan ✐ your response to the exam-style question below.

Exam-style question

Study **Figure 3**, which shows Old Harry Rocks, Handfast Point, Dorset.

i   Landform Z is a stack. Explain how a stack is formed.   **(4 marks)**

Figure 3

How confident do you feel about each of these **skills**? Colour ✐ in the bars.

① How do I write a good description of geographical processes?

② How can I improve my use of geographical language?

③ How do I write a good explanation of geographical processes?

④ Making the most of graph questions

This unit will help you learn how to work with graphs, by plotting, labelling, interpreting and describing different types of graph. The skills you will build are to:

- plot and read data on compound bar graphs
- interpret and plot data points on multiple-line graphs
- identify relationships and add lines of best fit to scatter graphs.

In the exam, you will come across a variety of graphs and will be asked to practise your graphical and geographical skills, such as labelling, plotting and interpreting data. This unit will prepare you to respond to exam questions based on graphs like the one below. This is a scatter graph.

Exam-style question

Study **Figure 1**, which shows a scatter graph of people with access to clean water and life expectancy in 12 countries.

i Plot Cameroon and Algeria on **Figure 1**, using the data in the table below. **(2 marks)**

Country	Access to clean water (%)	Life expectancy (years)
Cameroon	75	55
Algeria	85	75

ii Draw a line of best fit on **Figure 1**. **(1 mark)**

iii Describe the relationship between access to clean water and life expectancy shown in **Figure 1**. **(2 marks)**

iv Give **one** reason for the relationship shown in **Figure 1**. **(1 mark)**

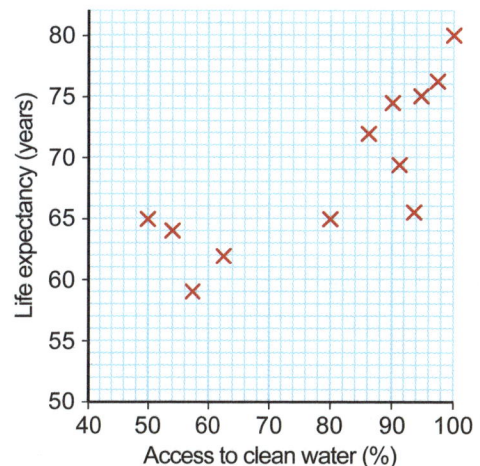

Figure 1

The three key questions in the **skill boosts** will help you to develop your confidence in answering questions based on graphs.

① How do I plot and read data on graphs?

② How do I interpret and plot data points on graphs?

③ How do I identify and show relationships on graphs?

A graph is a diagram showing how two or more sets of values are related. Most graphs have two axes – the horizontal line is the x-axis and the vertical line is the y-axis. Look at this exam-style question.

Exam-style question

Study **Figure 2**, which shows a scatter graph of people with access to clean water and child deaths in 12 countries.

i Label the data points for Madagascar and China on **Figure 2**, using the data in the table below.   **(2 marks)**

Country	Access to clean water (%)	Child deaths per 1000
Madagascar	50	53
China	94	12

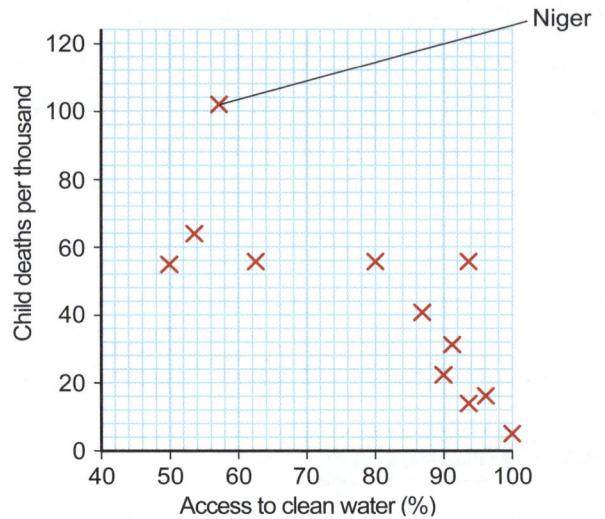

Figure 2

Each data point (✗) represents a country.

---

1 Note ✏ down what:

   a The graph shows

   ....

   ....

   b The x-axis shows

   ....

   c The y-axis shows

   ....

2 Underline (A) the command word and circle (A) the marks in the exam-style question.

When you look up data on a graph, read along the x-axis first and then up the y-axis (go along the corridor and then up the stairs). Look at **Figure 3** to see how the data point for Niger was plotted.

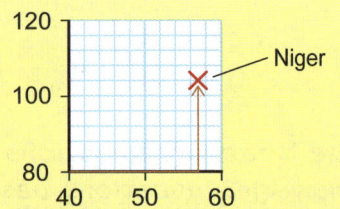

Figure 3 Niger data point

3 Now complete part i of the exam-style question above. Label the data points by drawing a ruled line from the (✗) and adding the country name ✏. Niger is an example of what you should do.

Labels identify what a feature is on a graph, map or photo. They are usually short – for example, a name (Niger) or a geographical term.

1 How do I plot and read data on graphs?

Figure 4 is a **compound bar graph**. This graph is divided to show the percentage share of three different economic sectors. You can plot and read data on compound bar graphs by following three simple steps.

> **Compound bar graph:** A bar graph divided into different sections stacked on top of each other, usually adding up to 100%.

Look at this exam-style question.

Exam-style question

Study **Figure 4**, a graph showing the changing distribution of GDP by economic sector in India, 1980–2011.

i Complete the compound bar graph in **Figure 4** for the year 1980–81, using the data in **Figure 5**.

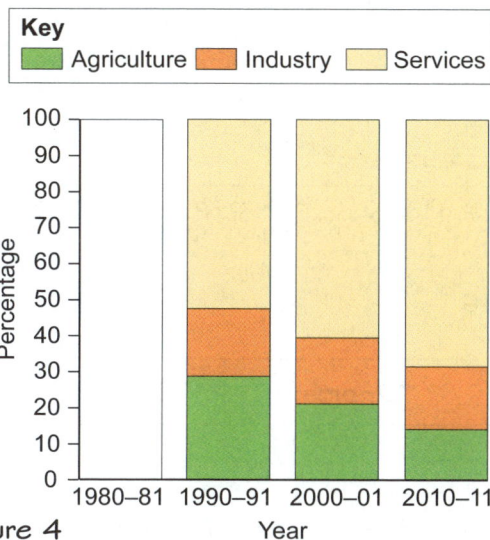

Figure 4

GDP by sector	Agriculture	Industry	Services
1980–81	36%	18%	46%
2010–11			

Figure 5

When you **plot** a compound bar graph, work through these steps:

Step 1: Start at 0 on the *y*-axis. Plot the top of the bar for the first sector (36%) with a line – use a sharp pencil and ruler.

Step 2: Add the bar for the second sector on top of the first (36% + 18% = 54%).

Step 3: Check the final sector adds up to 100% (54% + 46% = 100%), then shade all three sectors to match the key.

1 Use the steps above to plot ✏ a compound bar graph for 1980–81 on **Figure 4**, using the data in **Figure 5**.

> Use a clear ruler lined up with the *y*-axis to help you plot and read the data accurately.

When you **read** data from a compound bar graph, work through these steps:

Step 1: Read the *y*-axis value of the first (bottom) sector. For 1990–91, for example, the value = 28%.

Step 2: Read the *y*-axis value of the second sector, then take off the value of the first (47% − 28% = 19%).

Step 3: Read the *y*-axis value of the third sector, then take off the value of the first and second (100% − 47% = 53%).

2 Study **Figure 4** again. Read the data for agriculture, industry and services in 2010–11, then add ✏ the data to the table in **Figure 5**.

2 How do I interpret and plot data points on graphs?

A **multiple-line graph,** like the one below, has two or more lines plotted on the same axes. Always check the key so that you are sure what each line on the graph shows.

Look at this exam-style question and **Figure 6**, showing India's imports and exports, 1995–2013.

Exam-style question

i   Identify the value of India's imports in $US billion in 2008.   **(1 mark)**

☒ A   205 $US billion

☒ B   250 $US billion

☒ C   300 $US billion

☒ D   450 $US billion

ii   State the year that India's exports were $US125 billion.   **(1 mark)**

iii   Plot India's imports and exports in 2014 on **Figure 6**, using the data in the table below.   **(2 marks)**

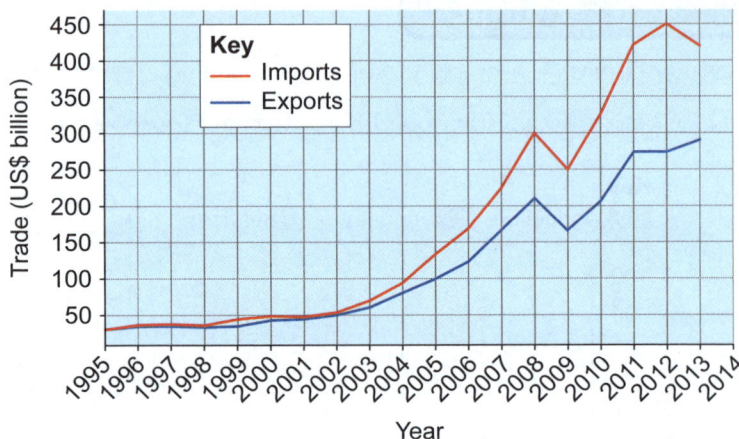

Figure 6

2014	Imports: US $420 billion	Exports: US $330 billion

(1) Check the labels on the *x*- and *y*-axes and the key. Now practise your skills by answering exam question parts i and ii above.

i   Cross ⊗ your response.

ii   Write ✎ your answer here. ....

Remember: To find a data point, first read along the *x*-axis and then up the *y*-axis.

(2) If you are asked to **plot** or **draw** data, you need to work directly on a graph, map or diagram. You also need to be accurate – so use a sharp pencil and a ruler.

a   Plot ✎ India's imports and exports in 2014 on **Figure 6**. Use the data in the table above.

b   Now draw ✎ the line graphs for India's imports and exports from 2013 to 2014.

(3) You might be asked about the **trend** in a graph. The phrases below can be used in sentences to describe trends.

Trend: The general direction of change.

Increased slowly	Increased rapidly	Dropped	Peaked	Fell slightly

Using these phrases and the information in **Figure 6**, write ✎ two sentences about the trend in India's imports.

....

....

3 How do I identify and show relationships on graphs?

In geography, a relationship or link between the values on the axes of a graph is called a **correlation**. Scatter graphs are good for checking to see if there is a correlation.

1. Look at the data points on the scatter graph, **Figure 7**.

Which of the phrases below describes the relationship between GDP and life expectancy? Tick it.

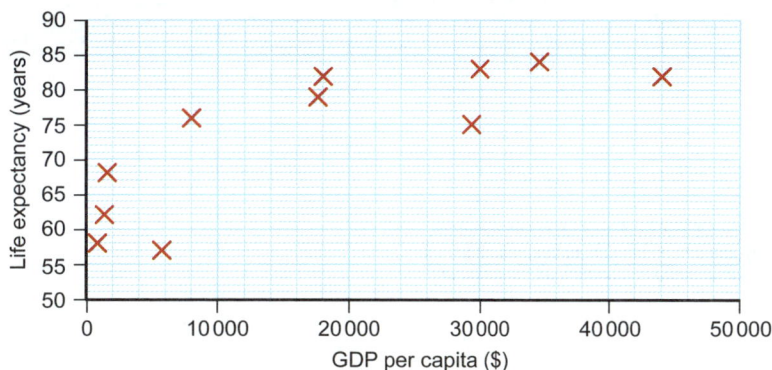

Figure 7 GDP per capita and life expectancy in 2015

As GDP increases, life expectancy decreases.	As life expectancy increases, GDP decreases.	As GDP increases, life expectancy increases.	There is no overall pattern in the data.
☐	☐	☐	☐

One way to check if there is a relationship between values is to draw a **line of best fit** through the data points. Look at **Figure 8**.

When you plot a line of best fit on a scatter graph:
- look for the overall trend and then place a ruler across the graph
- aim for the same number of data points on each side of your ruler
- draw your line of best fit.

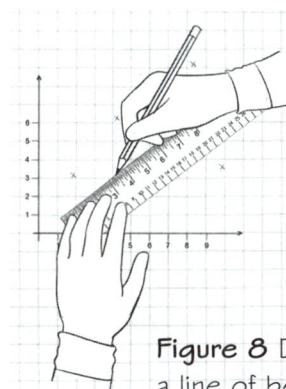

2. Now draw a line of best fit through the data points on **Figure 7**.

Figure 8 Drawing a line of best fit

3. Study **Figure 9**, which shows different types of correlation.

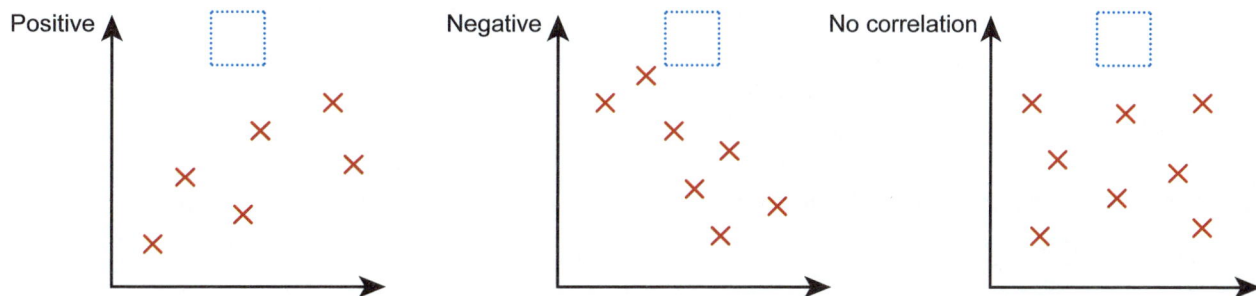

Positive   Negative   No correlation

Figure 9 Types of correlation

a. Which type of correlation does the scatter graph in **Figure 7** show? Tick it.

b. Write a sentence or two on paper, about the relationship shown in **Figure 7**, including the type of correlation you have identified.

Sample response

To work well with graph questions, you should:

- use a sharp pencil and ruler to plot, label and read data points
- use the rule 'along the x-axis and then up the y-axis'
- with scatter graphs, recognise the relationship or correlation between two sets of data – this can be positive or negative, or there may be no relationship.

Now look again at the graph below, which you first saw on page 26, and this exam-style question.

Exam-style question

Study **Figure 2**, which shows a scatter graph of people with access to clean water and child deaths in 12 countries.

i Draw a line of best fit on **Figure 2**. (1 mark)

ii Describe the relationship between access to clean water and child deaths shown in **Figure 2**. Use data from the graph to support your answer. (2 marks)

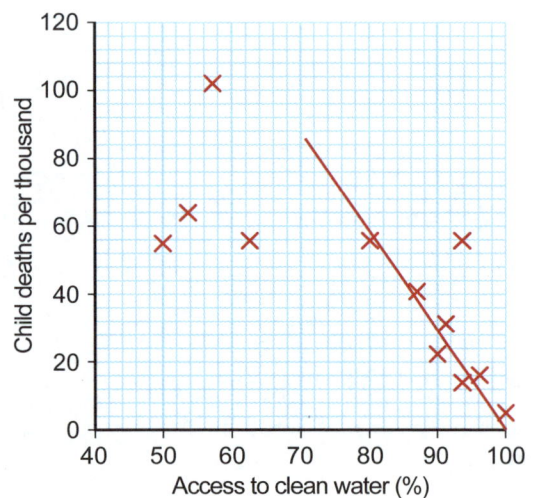

Figure 2

Sunita drew a **line of best fit** on **Figure 2** (see red line), and wrote a response to part ii below.

ii Figure 2 and the line of best fit show a negative relationship between access to clean water and child deaths. This means that as one goes up so does the other, meaning as countries get cleaner water, fewer children die. For example, the country with 100% clean water has child deaths of about 5%. Mainly the poorer countries have higher child deaths.

① Look again at Sunita's **line of best fit** on **Figure 2**. Then highlight 🖊 the good points in her response to part ii above, and underline Ⓐ any weaknesses.

② How would you improve on Sunita's answer?

ⓐ Draw 🖊 your line of best fit on **Figure 2** above.

ⓑ Rewrite 🖊 Sunita's description of the relationship shown in her response above.

....

....

....

Your turn!

You are now going to write your response to this exam-style question.

Exam-style question

Study **Figure 1**, which shows a scatter graph of people with access to clean water and life expectancy in 12 countries.

i   Plot Cameroon and Algeria on **Figure 1**, using the data in the table below.   **(2 marks)**

Country	Access to clean water (%)	Life expectancy (years)
Cameroon	75	55
Algeria	85	75

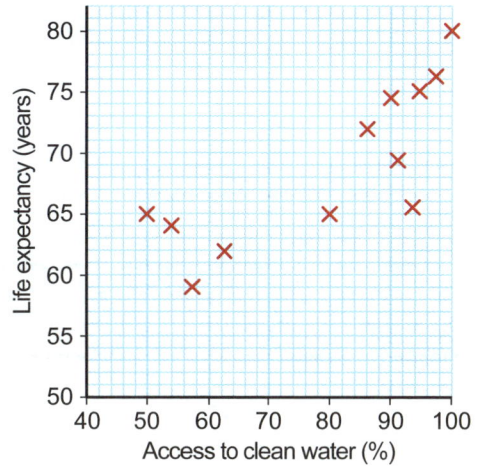

Figure 1

ii   Draw a line of best fit on **Figure 1**.   **(1 mark)**

iii Describe the relationship between access to clean water and life expectancy shown in **Figure 1**.   **(2 marks)**

iv   Give **one** reason for the relationship shown in **Figure 1**.   **(1 mark)**

① Plot/draw ✎ the answers to parts i and ii on **Figure 1** above.

② Write ✎ your answers to parts iii and iv below.

iii ....

....

....

iv ....

....

③ Review your responses to parts iii and iv.

   a Highlight ✎ the good points in your response.

   b Note ✎ down any improvements you could make below.

Review your skills

Check up

Review your response to the exam-style question on page 31. Tick ✓ the column to show how well you think you have done each of the following.

	Not quite ✓	Nearly there ✓	Got it! ✓
identified and labelled data on graphs	☐	☐	☐
plotted lines and data on graphs	☐	☐	☐
added lines of best fit and identified relationships on scatter graphs	☐	☐	☐

Look over all your work in this unit. Note ✎ down the **three** most important things you need to remember when working with graphs in geography.

① ....

② ....

③ ....

Need more practice?

Have a go at this exam-style question. ✎

Exam-style question

Compare the patterns and relationships in the data shown in **Figure 1** (page 25), people with access to clean water and life expectancy, and **Figure 2** (page 26), people with access to clean water and child deaths.

(3 marks)

For a **compare** question like this, you need to write about the data in **both graphs**, and say how they are similar and different. Use conjunctions (e.g. but, however, although) to help you structure your writing.

How confident do you feel about each of these **skills**? Colour ✎ in the bars.

① How do I plot and read data on graphs?
☐ ☐ ☐ ☐

② How do I interpret and plot data points on graphs?
☐ ☐ ☐ ☐

③ How do I identify and show relationships on graphs?
☐ ☐ ☐ ☐

⑤ Tackling numerical and statistical questions

This unit will help you understand how to use data to show geographical patterns. The skills that you will build are to:

• use numbers to calculate percentage change and ratio

• use statistical techniques to calculate midpoints and spread in a set of data

• make geographical conclusions from data.

In the exam, you will be asked to use data to make calculations and to analyse the geographical patterns that the data show. This unit will prepare you to respond to these questions.

Analyse the data in **Figure 1**, which shows data for urban areas in central Lagos, Nigeria.

Exam-style question

i   Calculate the percentage increase in the population size of Mushin between 2006 and 2015.   **(1 mark)**

ii Calculate the ratio of the population of Ajeromi-Ifelodun to the population of Apapa in 2006.   **(1 mark)**

iii Explain **two** reasons why population growth may affect the quality of life of people in Lagos.   **(4 marks)**

Area of central Lagos	Population 2006 (million)	Population 2015 (million)	Estimated daily solid waste generated 2015 (tonnes/day)
Ajeromi-Ifelodun	1.44	1.91	1203
Apapa	0.52	0.69	435
Lagos Island	0.86	1.14	718
Lagos Mainland	0.63	0.84	529
Mushin	1.32	1.76	1109
Shomolu	1.00	1.36	857
Surulere	1.27	1.69	1065

Figure 1

Exam-style question

i   Find the median value for the estimated daily solid waste generated in central Lagos in 2015.   **(1 mark)**

ii Calculate the inter-quartile range for the data on daily solid waste generated.   **(2 marks)**

iii Explain **one** reason why the amount of solid waste generated in Lagos in 2015 is likely to be higher than the amount generated in 2006.   **(2 marks)**

The three key questions in the **skills boosts** will help you to develop your numeracy and statistical skills.

① How do I do basic calculations using the data provided?

② How do I do statistical calculations using the data provided?

③ How do I identify geographical patterns within data?

In the exam, data may be provided for many topics. Look at **Figure 2**, which shows the peak flow discharge of the River Tees at Middleton, Teesdale, and one student's response to the exam-style question.

Exam-style question

Year	2010–11	2011–12	2012–13	2013–14	2014–15
Cumecs (m³/s)	261	282	260	178	167

Figure 2

i   Calculate the range in the peak flow discharge of the River Tees over these 5 years.   (1 mark)

ii Explain **one** reason why 2014–15 may have been a more difficult year for farmers in the valley of Teesdale. Use data to support your answer.   (2 marks)

Use maths to work out the answer.

Calculate: Produce a numerical answer, showing relevant working.

This is also good practice for **all** numerical questions, to reduce careless mistakes.

① Annabel worked out her answer to exam-style question part **i** to be:

i   Range: 261 – 167 = 94 m³/s.

Range: The difference between the highest and lowest data values. It measures the spread of the data.

Annabel correctly identified the lowest value (167 m³/s) but not the highest. She appears to have chosen the first and last values from **Figure 2** and perhaps got the lowest value by accident. This is a common error, so be careful to avoid it.

Remember to take your calculator into the exam.

What is the highest value in **Figure 2**? Calculate 🖊 the correct answer to exam-style question part **i**.

....

② Now look at Annabel's response to exam-style question part ii and her use of data.

2014–15 had the lowest peak discharge (167 cumecs) with a range of 94 cumecs. This means that farmers may not have had enough water for their animals or to irrigate their crops.

a Which data has Annabel used correctly to support her explanation? Circle Ⓐ it . Write 🖊 a sentence explaining your choice.

....

....

b Which data does **not** help support her explanation? Underline Ⓐ it . Write 🖊 a sentence explaining your choice.

....

....

1   **How do I do basic calculations using the data provided?**

When you are given a calculation to do, you must know which maths method to use. So make sure that you understand the terminology linked to numerical and statistical questions.

Worked example: Percentage increase

Look at the data below, which is an extract from **Figure 1** on page 33. Calculate the percentage increase in the population size of Apapa between 2006 and 2015.

Area of central Lagos	Population 2006 (million)	Population 2015 (million)
Apapa	0.52	0.69
Surulere	1.27	1.69

$$\text{percentage change} = \frac{\text{actual change}}{\text{original amount}} \times 100$$

$$\text{actual change} = \text{2015 value} - \text{2006 value}$$

$$= 0.69 - 0.52 = 0.17 \text{ million}$$

$$\text{percentage change} = \frac{0.17}{0.52} \times 100$$

$$= +32.69\% \text{ (to 2 d.p.)}$$

> Use your calculator.

> Unless stated otherwise, always give your answer to 2 decimal places (d.p.).

1 Calculate 🖊 the percentage increase in the population size of Surulere between 2006 and 2015. Show your working on paper.

Worked example: Ratio

Look at the data (see right), which is an extract from **Figure 1** on page 33. Calculate the ratio of the population of Lagos Island to the population of Lagos Mainland in 2015.

Area of central Lagos	Population 2015 (million)
Lagos Island	1.14
Lagos Mainland	0.84
Mushin	1.76
Shomolu	1.36

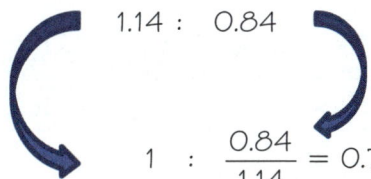

Island : Mainland

1.14 : 0.84

÷ 1.14   ÷ 1.14

$$1 : \frac{0.84}{1.14} = 0.7368...$$

Ratio is 1 : 0.74 (to 2 d.p.)

> A ratio compares the relative sizes of two values.

> Divide by the left-hand value to get 1 on the left-hand side of the ratio.

> Ratios are often in the form of 1 : n and they do not have any units.

2 Calculate 🖊 the ratio of the population of Mushin to the population of Shomolu in 2015. Show your working on paper.

2 How do I do statistical calculations using the data provided?

Statistical calculations often involve several steps, and care is needed at each step to make sure that the final answer is accurate. One of these calculations is finding the **inter-quartile range**.

Inter-quartile range: A way of showing the spread (or dispersion) of data by calculating the top and bottom of the middle section of a data set.

Look at **Figure 1** on page 33, which shows data for urban areas in central Lagos, Nigeria.

> ### Worked example: Median and inter-quartile range
>
> Using the population data for 2006, find the median and calculate the inter-quartile range.
>
> **Step 1:** Are the values in numerical order? If not, put them in order from high to low:
>
> 1.44   1.32   1.27   1.00   0.86   0.63   0.52
>
> **Step 2:** Find the **median**. This is the middle value in the order.
>
> 1.44   1.32   1.27   **1.00**   0.86   0.63   0.52
>
> **Step 3:** Find the **upper quartile**. Look at the top half of the data (values above the median). Here, there are three values. Find the middle value of the top half.
>
> 1.44   **1.32**   1.27   **1.00**   0.86   0.63   0.52
>
> **Step 4:** Find the **lower quartile**. Look at the bottom half of the data (values below the median). Here, there are three values. Find the middle value of the bottom half.
>
> 1.44   **1.32**   1.27   **1.00**   0.86   **0.63**   0.52
>
> **Step 5:** Calculate the **inter-quartile range**. This is the difference between the **upper quartile** and the **lower quartile**. So for 2006, this is:
>
> 1.44   **1.32**   1.27   **1.00**   0.86   **0.63**   0.52
>
> upper quartile − lower quartile = 1.32 − 0.63 = 0.69 million.

① Isabel used the data in **Figure 1** page 33 to find the median and calculate the inter-quartile range of the population for areas of central Lagos in 2015.

Median = 1.36 million ☐

Inter-quartile range = 1.22 million ☐

Use the data to find the median and calculate ✎ the inter-quartile range for yourself. Show your working on paper. Then mark Isabel's answers with a tick ✓ or a cross ✗.

> ### Worked example: Even numbers of data values
>
> Find the median pebble size in the following data:
>
> | Pebble size (mm) | | | | | | | |
> |---|---|---|---|---|---|---|---|
> | 10 | 8 | 11 | 6 | 3 | 14 | 7 | 5 |
>
> **Step 1:** 14   11   10   **8**   **7**   6   5   3 ◁ Place data in numerical order.
>
> **Step 2:**
>
> $$\text{median} = \frac{8 + 7}{2} = 7.5 \text{ mm}$$
>
> Calculate the **mean** (average) of the two middle values.

② Now calculate ✎ the inter-quartile range of the pebble sizes. Show your working on paper.

To find the lower quartile, you need to calculate the mean of 6 and 5. Apply the same method to find the upper-quartile value.

3 How do I identify geographical patterns within data?

In the exam, you may be asked to show your geographical understanding of a topic based on your studies **and** the data provided with a question, including any calculations you may have done.

Look at this exam-style question and the survey results for two rivers in England between 2010 and 2015.

Exam-style question

	Highest peak discharge (m³/s)	Lowest peak discharge (m³/s)	Ratio of highest : lowest	Range (m³/s)	Mean (m³/s)	Median (m³/s)	Inter-quartile range (m³/s)
River Tees	282	167	1 : 0.59	115	229.6	260	83
River Gipping	27	11	1 : 0.41	16	17.2	16	4

Figure 3

Suggest **two** reasons for the differences between the discharges of the River Tees and the River Gipping. **(4 marks)**

Here, you need to identify geographical patterns within the data. To write an effective response, you need to include relevant data from the table (or other source) provided and/or any calculations you have completed, use geographical language, and show geographical understanding of the topic.

Now read Grahame's response to the exam-style question above.

> The River Tees has a peak discharge over 10 times greater than the River Gipping. The inter-quartile range also shows that the River Tees has a greater variation in peak discharges. These differences could be due to the rock type. The River Gipping could have more permeable rock so that any rainfall soaks away while in the River Tees area it runs off the surface into the river. The discharges could also be different because the River Tees area has much higher precipitation than the River Gipping area.

① How effective is Grahame's response and use of data? Circle Ⓐ his use of relevant data. Underline Ⓐ his use of geographical language. Highlight ✐ where he shows some geographical understanding of the topic.

Sometimes questions may ask you to show your understanding of the **reliability** of data.

② Read through these factors which can affect the reliability of data.

Very large sample size	☐	High-quality equipment used	☐
Data collected over a long time period	☐	Small sample size	☐
Equipment failure or inaccuracy	☐	Planned sampling methods	☐
Data collected over a short time period	☐	Estimated data	☐

Tick ✓ all the reasons that may lead to **unreliable** data.

Sample response

To do well in numerical or statistical questions, you should be able to:

- do basic calculations using the data provided
- use the data provided to carry out statistical calculations
- show your understanding of geographical patterns and the reliability of data.

Now look again at the data in **Figure 1** on page 33 and the exam-style question below.

Exam-style question

i   Find the median value for the estimated daily solid waste generated in central Lagos in 2015. **(1 mark)**

ii Calculate the inter-quartile range for the data on daily solid waste generated. **(2 marks)**

iii Explain **one** reason why the amount of solid waste generated in Lagos in 2015 is likely to be higher than the amount generated in 2006. **(2 marks)**

(1) Look at Annabel and Grahame's responses to question parts **i** and **ii**.

Annabel

i 529 tonnes/day	☐
ii Upper quartile = 1109 t/d, lower quartile = 529 t/d so inter-quartile range is 580 t/d	☐

Grahame

i 857	☐
ii Lower quartile = 529, upper quartile = 1109, so inter-quartile range is 580	☐

Use the data to find the median and calculate ✏ the inter-quartile range for yourself. Show your working on paper. Then mark the students' answers with a tick ✓ or a cross ✗.

(2) Now look at Annabel and Grahame's responses to question part **iii**.

Annabel

iii It will be higher because the population of Mushin has grown by a third, so more people means that more waste will be created. ☐

Grahame

iii It's higher because people have become wealthier and so buy more products and everything has more packaging. ☐

a Use colour-coding ✏ to highlight each student's key point, their use of numbers or statistics and any reasons or explanations they have given.

b Underline Ⓐ or strike through ~~cat~~ any parts that don't work well.

c There are 2 marks for this question. Which is the most effective response? Tick ✓ it.

d Write ✏ a sentence or two on paper explaining your choice.

Your turn!

You are now going to write your own response to this exam-style question.

Exam-style question

Analyse the data in **Figure 1**, which shows data for urban areas in central Lagos, Nigeria.

Area of central Lagos	Population 2006 (million)	Population 2015 (million)	Estimated daily solid waste generated 2015 (tonnes/day)
Ajeromi-Ifelodun	1.44	1.91	1203
Apapa	0.52	0.69	435
Lagos Island	0.86	1.14	718
Lagos Mainland	0.63	0.84	529
Mushin	1.32	1.76	1109
Shomolu	1.00	1.36	857
Surulere	1.27	1.69	1065

Figure 1

i Calculate the percentage increase in the population size of Mushin between 2006 and 2015.

(1 mark)

ii Calculate the ratio of the population of Ajeromi-Ifelodun to the population of Apapa in 2006.

(1 mark)

iii Explain **two** reasons why population growth may affect the quality of life of people in Lagos.

(4 marks)

① Calculate 🖉 the answer to question part **i**. Show your working.

② Calculate 🖉 your answer to question part **ii**. Show your working.

③ Look at exam-style question part **iii**. Underline Ⓐ any key phrases in the question. Then quickly jot 🖉 down some notes on paper.

④ Now write 🖉 your response to exam-style question part **iii** on paper, using **Point – Development** to structure your writing (see Unit 2). Make sure that you use numerical or statistical information in your answer.

Review your skills

Check up

Review your response to the exam-style question on page 39. Tick ✓ the relevant column boxes to show how well you think you have done each of the following:

	Not quite ✓	Nearly there ✓	Got it! ✓
made basic calculations using the data provided	☐	☐	☐
used the data to carry out statistical calculations	☐	☐	☐
explained geographical patterns and the reliability of data	☐	☐	☐

Look over all of your work in this unit. Note 🖉 down the **three** most important things that you will need to remember when faced with numerical or statistical questions.

① ....

② ....

③ ....

Need more practice?

Study the numerical and statistical instructions and commands. Match them to the correct 'what it tells you to do' by drawing 🖉 a line from the left column to the matching statement on the right.

Instruction or command

- Calculate the range
- Calculate the ratio of
- Calculate the percentage increase/decrease
- Suggest **two** reasons
- Calculate the inter-quartile range
- Find the median

What it tells you to do

- Divide the lower value being compared by the higher value. Write the answer in the form 1 : n, where the higher value = 1.
- Highest value minus lowest value
- The middle value in a list of numbers placed in numerical order
- Middle value of the top half of the data minus middle value of the lower half of the data
- Give explanations for geographical patterns within data.
- $\frac{actual\ change}{original\ amount} \times 100$

How confident do you feel about each of these **skills**? Colour 🖉 in the bars.

❶ How do I do basic calculations using the data provided? ☐☐☐☐

❷ How do I do statistical calculations using the data provided? ☐☐☐☐

❸ How do I identify geographical patterns within data? ☐☐☐☐

Get started

Apply knowledge and understanding to interpret, analyse and evaluate geographical information and issues and to make judgements (AO3)

⑥ Getting to grips with assess questions

This unit will help you learn how to structure answers to questions which use 'assess' as the command word. The skills you will build are to:

- identify relevant geographical ideas
- develop your ideas using evidence
- write an effective conclusion that answers the question.

In the exam, you will be asked to tackle questions that require you to **assess** a situation or statement. You will be expected to use evidence to determine the relative significance of the topic that is being discussed. You will then need to consider all of the different factors and identify which are the most important.

Exam-style question

'The causes of coastal flooding are mainly a result of human activity.' Assess this statement.

(8 marks)

The three key questions in the **skills boosts** will help you to prepare your response to an 'assess' question.

① How do I identify relevant geographical ideas?

② How do I develop my ideas using evidence?

③ How do I write an effective conclusion that answers the question?

Look at one student's response to a similar task on the next page.

Exam-style question

For a named megacity in a developing or emerging country, assess the factors which affect quality of life. (8 marks)

Assess: Use evidence to determine the relative significance of something. Give consideration to all factors and identify which are the most important.

Mumbai is a megacity of 12.5 million people located in western India. The quality of life – the degree of well-being felt by people – varies across the city although generally it is lower than other megacities in emerging Asian countries. Mumbai is a relatively wealthy megacity which has high levels of foreign direct investment and yet its housing, health care, transport, sanitation and pollution are relatively poor.

There are several factors which affect the quality of life in Mumbai. Most of Mumbai's housing is rent-controlled which means that there is a limit to how high rents can be. So there is no incentive for people to improve their houses because they would get the same rents for the improved house as they currently have. There are also high levels of corruption so those areas which were meant to be developed were actually sold to property developers and converted into expensive apartment blocks which many people cannot afford.

The government is also inefficient and bureaucratic so it takes a long time for improvements to happen. Consequently, new houses often have to wait for sanitation and waste disposal to be provided. Adequate sanitation and waste disposal can dramatically improve people's quality of life. In Dharavi, a slum in Mumbai, over 500 people share each public latrine so most people go to the toilet in streams which run through the settlement.

Lack of adequate sanitation and waste disposal is probably the most important factor affecting quality of life because if the water supply is highly polluted, this can cause diseases, such as cholera, which can be fatal and trap people into a cycle of poverty.

There are several key elements to an effective response to an 'assess' question.

(1) Look carefully at Chris's response above, thinking about each of the elements below. Tick ✓ the elements that you think he has done well.

He has clearly introduced his megacity.	☐	The megacity is in a developing or emerging country.	☐
He has identified several factors which affect the quality of life in his named megacity.	☐	He has used data to illustrate these factors.	☐
He has explained why these factors affect the quality of life in his megacity.	☐	He has used geographical language and connectives to make good points.	☐
He has identified which of the factors is the most important.	☐	He has explained why he thinks this factor is the most important.	☐

(2) Write ✏ one or two sentences commenting on the overall effectiveness of Chris's response.

....

....

....

....

1 How do I identify relevant geographical ideas?

It is important in an exam that you don't just write everything you know about a topic. You need to identify relevant geographical ideas and determine the relative significance of each one to the topic.

Look again at this exam-style question.

Exam-style question

For a named megacity in a developing or emerging country, assess the factors which affect quality of life. **(8 marks)**

Quality of life: The degree of well-being (physical and psychological) felt by an individual or a group of people in a particular area. This may relate to jobs, wages, food and access to services such as health and education.

① Before you can assess the factors which affect quality of life, you first need to identify them. Think about all the different factors that come to mind when you think about this topic. Add ✏️ at least **four** to the spider diagram below.

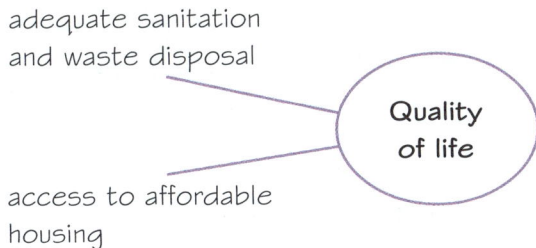

adequate sanitation and waste disposal

Quality of life

access to affordable housing

② Now think about the relative significance of the factors below to quality of life. Which of the following statements do you think are the most important? Number ✏️ the statements, with **1** for the most significant down to **5** for the least significant.

The government is inefficient and bureaucratic so it takes a long time for improvements to happen.

Mumbai is a relatively wealthy megacity which has high levels of foreign direct investment.

Adequate sanitation and waste disposal can dramatically improve people's quality of life.

A rapid rise in private cars means that Mumbai's roads are frequently gridlocked, leading to 'super dense' traffic congestions.

The majority of employment in Mumbai is in the 'informal sector', which means that working conditions are poor.

③ Finally, think about **your** factors. Which ones do **you** think significantly affect quality of life? Write ✏️ a sentence or two summing them up.

....

....

....

....

2 How do I develop my ideas using evidence?

When you discuss your geographical ideas, you are aiming to determine the relative significance of each one to the topic and to identify which are the most important. To achieve this, you can use **PEEL** to structure your response:

- **P**oint – make a statement about each of your geographical ideas.
- **E**vidence – provide some data, facts or examples to show the value of each point.
- **E**xplanation – focus on reasons and explanations for each point.
- **L**ink – link the point back to the question.

> If the question asks for a **named example**, then you **must** include evidence specific to this example.

① Evidence can take the form of statistics, data, generally accepted facts and/or examples, such as the following.

A Currently there are over 1.8 million cars in Mumbai.	**B** Over 60% of the population of Mumbai work in the informal sector.
C Mumbai's growth has been too rapid for local government to organise waste disposal. Instead this is run by small-scale businesses.	**D** 40% of India's exports come from Mumbai, and it is India's top location for foreign direct investment.

Now look at these key points. Which piece of evidence, **A**, **B**, **C** or **D**, best supports each one? Add ✏ the letter of your chosen evidence to the table below.

	Key points	Evidence
1	The majority of employment in Mumbai is in the 'informal sector'.	
2	A rapid rise in private cars means that Mumbai's roads are frequently gridlocked.	
3	Mumbai is a relatively wealthy megacity with high levels of foreign direct investment.	
4	The government is inefficient and bureaucratic so it takes a long time for improvements to happen.	

② Now look at this key point:

> Lack of adequate sanitation is a factor which affects people's quality of life.

Write ✏ a sentence or two, giving evidence to support it. Use Chris's response on page 42 to help you, or any other facts or examples you know about a named megacity in a developing or emerging country.

....

....

....

....

3 **How do I write an effective conclusion that answers the question?**

Once you have considered all of the factors, you then need to identify which are the most important. You can use your **conclusion** to identify your choice. An effective conclusion should emphasise your ideas, not simply repeat them. Linking back to the question in your conclusion can help you to stay on track.

Look again at the exam-style question on page 42 and remind yourself of the definition of 'assess'.

1 Look back at the factors you identified on page 43. Note 🖉 down **three** factors that you might want to write about in response to the exam-style question and one or two pieces of evidence for each one.

Factor	Evidence

2 Identify the factor you think is the **most** important in affecting people's quality of life in your named megacity. Tick it ✓. Write 🖉 one or two sentences explaining your choice.

....

....

3 Look again at Chris's response to the exam-style question on page 42 and his conclusion below.

> Lack of adequate sanitation and waste disposal is probably the most important factor affecting quality of life because if the water supply is highly polluted, this can cause diseases, such as cholera, which can be fatal and trap people into a cycle of poverty.

a In Chris's conclusion, underline Ⓐ and label 🖉 where:

  i he repeats his key point (reread his response on page 42 if you need to)

  ii he emphasises a key idea without repeating it

  iii he links back to the question.

b Note 🖉 down **one** way Chris could improve his conclusion.

....

....

Sample response

To write a clear response to an 'assess' question, you should:

- identify relevant geographical ideas
- develop your ideas using evidence
- write an effective conclusion that answers the question.

Look again at the exam-style question, which you saw at the start of the unit.

Exam-style question

'The causes of coastal flooding are mainly a result of human activity.' Assess this statement.

(8 marks)

Now read Sara's response to the exam-style question.

> Coastal flooding is when low-lying land which is normally dry is flooded with seawater. There are several physical reasons why this can happen. Strong winds can push the water onto the coastline to create a storm surge. This often happens during hurricanes or cyclones. Global warming can also cause sea levels to rise which can flood low-lying land.
>
> However, human activity is also important. In some places people have re-claimed land from the sea and it is often found below sea-level. Also, humans have changed the processes in other places along the coast by putting in hard and soft engineering. This can protect some parts of the coast but move the problem of erosion and flooding somewhere else. So, if groynes are put in somewhere to keep the beach in place there won't be a large beach down the coast, and this means the waves can get to the land more easily and flood it. People also build houses on the coast for a good sea view. If they didn't build it wouldn't matter so much if the land flooded but because they do, it can be very expensive if the coast does flood.
>
> In conclusion, I think that at the moment the causes of coastal flooding are mainly a result of human activity because they have made it more likely to cause damage. But in the future, if global warming increases and hurricanes happen more often, then I think that physical factors may be more important.

1 How effective is Sara's assessment of the causes of coastal flooding?

- **a** Highlight ✎ the different causes Sara has given for coastal flooding.
- **b** Underline Ⓐ the evidence she has provided to support each cause of coastal flooding.
- **c** Circle Ⓐ any reasons or explanations Sara has given for the causes of coastal flooding.
- **d** Look again at Sara's conclusion. Does she emphasise her ideas, not simply repeat them? Does she link back to the question? Tick ✓ it if you agree.

2 What advice would you give Sara to improve her answer? Note ✎ down two suggestions.

1 ....

....

2 ....

....

Your turn!

You are now going to write your response to this exam-style question.

Exam-style question

'The causes of coastal flooding are mainly a result of human activity.' Assess this statement.

(8 marks)

(1) Note ✏ down some causes of coastal flooding.

Human factors	Physical factors

(2) What evidence do you have to support the causes you have identified? Note ✏ down your evidence below.

Human	Physical

(3) From your evidence, can you determine whether coastal flooding is **mainly** a result of human activity or physical factors or both equally? Write ✏ a sentence or two explaining your choice.

....

....

....

....

(4) Now write ✏ your full response to the exam-style question on paper, thinking carefully about:

- giving reasons or explanations for each of the causes you mention
- identifying which is the most important cause
- linking back to the question in your conclusion.

Review your skills

Check up

Review your response to the exam-style question on page 47. Tick ✓ the column to show how well you think you have done each of the following.

	Not quite ✓	Nearly there ✓	Got it! ✓
identified relevant geographical ideas	☐	☐	☐
developed my ideas using evidence	☐	☐	☐
written an effective conclusion that answers the question	☐	☐	☐

Look over all of your work in this unit. Note ✏ down the **three** most important things to remember when assessing the relative significance of something.

① ....

② ....

③ ....

Need more practice?

Have a go at answering the exam-style question below and practise your timings. ✏

Exam-style question

Assess the role of human activity in climate change.   **(8 marks)**

Climate change: A long-term change in the Earth's climate, especially changes in temperature.

How confident do you feel about each of these **skills**? Colour ✏ in the bars.

❶ How do I identify relevant geographical ideas?

❷ How do I develop my ideas using evidence?

❸ How do I write an effective conclusion that answers the question?

Apply knowledge and understanding to interpret, analyse and evaluate geographical information and issues and to make judgements (AO3)

(7) Making effective evaluations

This unit will help you learn how to structure answers to questions which use 'evaluate' as the command word. The skills you will build are to:

* identify the strengths and weaknesses of the geographical idea identified in the question
* weigh up those strengths and weaknesses
* bring together information to form a conclusion and suggest alternatives.

In the exam, you will be asked to tackle questions that require you to **evaluate** something. This could be content you have studied, fieldwork or data. You will need to measure its success and provide a conclusion by weighing up the strengths and weaknesses, referring to data and suggesting alternatives. This unit will prepare you to write your own response to the following question.

Exam-style question

You have carried out your own fieldwork investigating an urban area.

Evaluate the reliability of your conclusions. (8 marks)

The three key questions in the **skills boosts** will help you to prepare your response to an 'evaluate' question.

1 How do I identify strengths and weaknesses?

2 How do I weigh up the strengths and weaknesses?

3 How do I write an effective evaluative conclusion?

Look at one student's response to a similar task on the next page.

Identifying what the question is asking you to do is one of the most important skills in answering exam questions. Look at this exam-style question.

Exam-style question

Evaluate different responses to the impacts of earthquakes in a named developed country.

(8 marks)

Look at the definition of 'evaluate'.

Review information, using evidence such as strengths, weaknesses, alternatives and relevant data.

Evaluate: Measure the value or success of something and ultimately provide a substantiated judgement/substantiated conclusion.

Make a decision based on all your evidence.

Form a conclusion by drawing together all your evidence.

① Now apply this definition to the exam-style question above.

a Note ✎ down what you need to measure the value or success of in the question.

....

b Note ✎ down how you will go about tackling this question.

....

....

Salma has also noted what she needs to do to answer the question. You can read this in the box below.

I need to look at how different people, organisations or governments have responded to the impacts of an earthquake and weigh up the strengths and weaknesses. In my conclusion, I will compare the success of each and suggest how responses to earthquakes could be improved. My case study is Japan.

② Compare your notes with Salma's, using the checklist below.

Checklist I have ...	⊘
correctly identified what needs to be evaluated	
identified how I will go about measuring the value or success of this	
suggested there may be alternatives/improvements	
identified how I will draw this together in my conclusion	
named a developed country.	

The earthquake you choose needs to be in a **developed country**. Double check that the earthquake you have chosen fits this requirement.

a Tick ✓ any features that are present in both your own and Salma's response.

b Note ✎ down anything that you have omitted and must remember to include in your response to the exam-style question.

....

....

1 How do I identify strengths and weaknesses?

In order to be able to measure the value or success of something, you must first identify the strengths and weaknesses.

Look again at this exam-style question.

Exam-style question

Evaluate different responses to the impacts of earthquakes in a named developed country.

(8 marks)

① Look at the statements and explanations below, which refer to the earthquake that shook north-east Japan and triggered a tsunami in 2011.

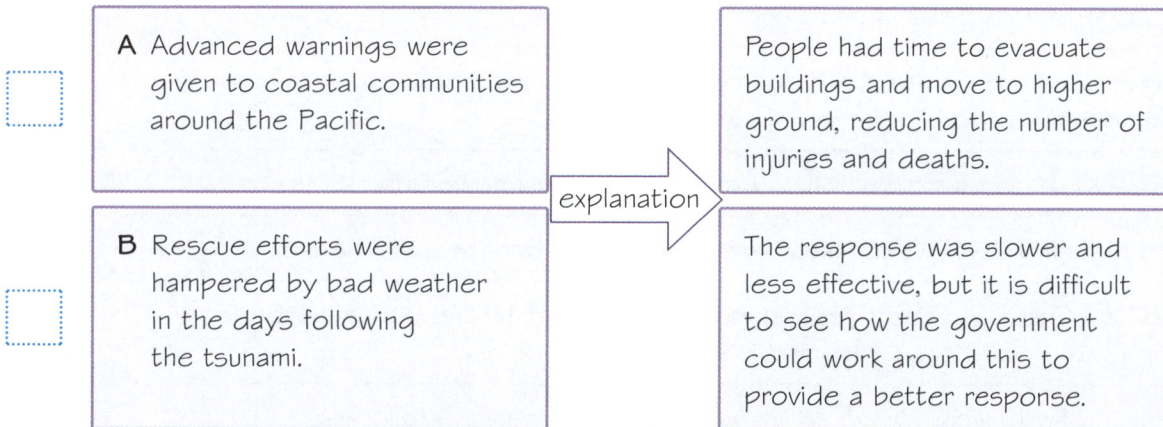

A Advanced warnings were given to coastal communities around the Pacific.	People had time to evacuate buildings and move to higher ground, reducing the number of injuries and deaths.
B Rescue efforts were hampered by bad weather in the days following the tsunami.	The response was slower and less effective, but it is difficult to see how the government could work around this to provide a better response.

explanation

Which statement describes a strength of the response and which describes a weakness? Label 🖋 **S** for strength and **W** for weakness.

A strength is likely to be well-coordinated and save lives, whereas a weakness may lead to delays and further loss of life.

② Now think about your chosen earthquake and the immediate and long-term responses.

ⓐ Write 🖋 down **two** strengths and **two** weaknesses of the responses.

Strengths	Weaknesses

ⓑ For each strength and weakness you have identified, write 🖋 a sentence or two on paper, explaining why it is a strength or a weakness.

2 How do I weigh up the strengths and weaknesses?

Once you have identified the strengths and weaknesses of something, you then need to weigh them up to see how successful the thing has been. Think of it as a pair of scales with strengths on one side and weaknesses on the other.

1 One way to weigh up the strengths and weaknesses is to use a scoring system. Look at some of the strengths and weaknesses of the responses to the 2011 Japan earthquake below.

Statement	Strength or weakness?	Score (10–1)
Advanced warnings were given to coastal communities around the Pacific by the Pacific Tsunami Warning Center.		
The Japanese government requested international aid from Australia, China, India, New Zealand and South Korea.		
There was disruption to roads and communications which made it difficult to get food to the people who needed it.		
140,000 people were evacuated from the Fukushima power plant.		
Tens of thousands of prefabricated temporary houses were set up in Sendai.		
The Red Cross and Red Crescent provided support to the government along with private companies and NGOs.		
Rescue efforts were hampered by bad weather in the days following the tsunami.		

a Which statements describe a strength of the response and which a weakness? Write ✎ S for strength and **W** for weakness.

b Give each statement a score. Note ✎ down a number between 1 and 10, where 10 is a strong strength or weakness and 1 is a weak strength or weakness.

There is no right or wrong answer to this exercise. However, a very strong response is likely to be well-coordinated and save lives.

2 Add up the scores for first the strengths and then the weaknesses and write ✎ them beside the scales.

It is important that you weigh up the strengths and weaknesses rather than just count how many there are of each. There may only be one strength and four weaknesses, but the weaknesses may be very small in comparison to a very important strength.

Strengths   Weaknesses

3 Which side of the scales has the higher score and is heavier? What does this tell you about the responses to the 2011 earthquake in Japan? Write ✎ one or two sentences below.

....

....

3   **How do I write an effective evaluative conclusion?**

A good conclusion to an evaluate question will explain the value or success of the thing that you have been considering (for example, the response to an earthquake) and suggest how it could be improved.

It does not matter if the thing you are evaluating has lots of weaknesses. In fact, the more it has the easier it is to write an interesting and effective conclusion. This is particularly important to remember if the exam question is about your own fieldwork.

① Look at Tabitha's conclusion to the exam-style question on page 50.

> In conclusion, the response to the .... earthquake was a success/failure.
>
> The government, private companies and NGOs responded quickly and effectively/slowly and
>
> ineffectively and there were many/few weaknesses in their response. One weakness was ....
>
> ....
>
> This could be improved by ....
>
> ....

Help her to complete it.

a Write 🖉 the name of an earthquake in a developed country.

b State whether, on balance, the responses were a success or a failure. Explain why. Strike through (~~eat~~) the words/phrases that do not apply.

c Note 🖉 down a weakness and suggest how this could be improved.

② You could be asked to evaluate more than one thing and to say which was more successful. Look at this exam-style question.

> **Exam-style question**
>
> Evaluate responses to the impacts of earthquakes in a named developed and developing country.   **(8 marks)**

Look at Gemma's conclusion to the exam-style question above.

> In conclusion, I think that the response to the Japanese earthquake was more effective than the response to the Haiti earthquake. The Japanese were prepared and had early warning systems but the Haitians are poor and were unprepared. Many people were trapped in buildings and it was difficult to rescue them because no one was in charge. The response to the Haiti earthquake would have been more effective if they had responded in a similar way to the Japanese. Retrofitting 'earthquake proof' technology would have stopped buildings from falling down and killing people.

How effective is Gemma's conclusion?

a Which earthquake did Gemma identify as having a more successful response? Circle Ⓐ it.

b Underline Ⓐ the explanation she has provided to support her choice.

c Highlight 🖉 a weakness of the response to one of the earthquakes and her suggestion for how this could be improved.

Sample response

To write a clear response to an 'evaluate' question, you should:

- identify the strengths and weaknesses of the thing you are considering
- weigh up those strengths and weaknesses
- write a conclusion that evaluates how successful the thing is and how it could be improved.

Look again at the exam-style question which you saw at the start of the unit.

Exam-style question

You have carried out your own fieldwork investigating an urban area.

Evaluate the reliability of your conclusion. **(8 marks)**

Here, **reliability** means how close the conclusion is to what is actually happening in the urban environment. The strengths and weaknesses you identify are the things that make the conclusions more or less reliable.

Now read Sasha's response to the exam-style question.

The conclusion to my fieldwork in Birmingham was that the quality of life in Sparkbrook ward was not as high as the quality of life in Ladywood ward. This is likely to be accurate as the secondary data from the census supported the observations that I made as I walked around the two areas. However, the sampling strategy that I used may have made the conclusion less reliable. I only did my environmental quality survey in three places and I might have missed other places that would have given me different results and a different conclusion. I also carried out my questionnaires at 2 pm on a Tuesday afternoon and it was raining. Therefore, there were lots of people I couldn't ask, for example school children who were probably in school, and some of the people who I did ask were rude and didn't want to answer because they didn't want to get wet. On balance, I think that my conclusion is fairly reliable. If I was going to do my fieldwork again I would make sure that I did my environmental quality survey in more places and I would also make sure that I did my questionnaires at different times so that I would get a more representative sample.

① How effective is Sasha's evaluation of the reliability of her urban fieldwork conclusion?

a Use colour-coding to highlight ✎ the strengths and weaknesses of her fieldwork.

b Underline Ⓐ where she has weighed up these strengths and weaknesses.

c Circle Ⓐ her conclusion to the exam-style question.

② Look again at Sasha's response to the exam-style question. Does she measure the reliability of her conclusion to her urban fieldwork and ultimately provide a substantiated judgement/conclusion? Note ✎ down what she does well and suggest **one** improvement she could make.

Sasha's response is good because ....

....

....

One way she could improve her response is by ....

....

....

Your turn!

You are now going to write your response to this exam-style question.

Exam-style question

You have carried out your own fieldwork investigating an urban area.

Evaluate the reliability of your conclusion.   (8 marks)

① Note ✐ down the strengths and weaknesses that make your fieldwork conclusion more or less reliable.

② Note ✐ down why they are strengths or weaknesses. Continue on paper if you run out of space.

Scores	Strengths/Weaknesses	Explanations

③ Now weigh up your strengths and weaknesses giving each a score of between 1 and 10, where 10 is a strong strength or weakness and 1 is a weak strength or weakness. Add them up and write ✐ them beside the scales.

Strengths   Weaknesses

④ Which has the higher score: the strengths or the weaknesses? What does this tell you about the reliability of your fieldwork conclusion? Note ✐ your ideas below.

⑤ How could you have improved your fieldwork to make your conclusion more reliable? Note ✐ one or two possibilities below.

⑥ Now write ✐ your response to the above exam-style question on paper.

Review your skills

Check up

Review your response to the exam-style question on page 55. Tick ✓ the column to show how well you think you have done each of the following.

	Not quite ✓	Nearly there ✓	Got it! ✓
identified the strengths and weaknesses	☐	☐	☐
weighed up the strengths and weaknesses	☐	☐	☐
written an effective evaluative conclusion and identified areas for improvement	☐	☐	☐

Look over all of your work in this unit. Note ✐ down the **three** most important things to remember when evaluating something.

① ....

② ....

③ ....

Need more practice?

Have a go at answering the exam-style question below and practise your timings. ✐

Exam-style question

You have carried out your own fieldwork investigating variations in the quality of life within urban areas. Name your urban environment fieldwork location:

....

Evaluate the relative importance of primary and secondary data in your investigation.　　(8 marks)

How confident do you feel about each of these **skills**? Colour ✐ in the bars.

❶ How do I identify strengths and weaknesses?

❷ How do I weigh up the strengths and weaknesses?

❸ How do I write an effective evaluative conclusion?

⑧ Justifying in geographical writing

This unit will help you learn how to make a geographical decision from a selection of choices, and then write paragraphs that justify the decision made. The skills that you will build are to:

- make a clear geographical decision based on evidence
- identify and include the strengths and weaknesses of each option
- write a detailed justification of a geographical decision.

In Paper 3 of the exam, you will be asked to look at several resources (diagrams, data, maps, photographs, graphs and/or text extracts) so that you can explore a geographical issue, challenge or problem. This unit will prepare you to write your own response to this question.

Exam-style question

Study the **three** options below for providing energy supplies over the next 30 years.

Option 1: Use mostly oil and other fossil fuels such as natural gas.

Option 2: Use mostly wind energy and other renewables such as solar power.

Option 3: Use a combination of oil and wind energy.

Select the option that you think would be best for meeting the energy needs of the world in the next 30 years. Justify your choice.

Use information from the Resource Booklet (pages 65–66) and knowledge and understanding from the rest of your geography course to support your answer.

(16 marks)

> 4 marks will be for your spelling, punctuation and grammar and use of specialist terminology.

The three key questions in the **skills boosts** will help you to develop your decision-making skills for the 'select and justify' question.

1 How do I support my geographical decision with evidence?

2 How do I identify the strengths and weaknesses of the options?

3 How do I write a justification of my geographical decision?

First look at the resources on pages 65–66 before continuing work on this unit.

> In the exam, the resources will be presented in a **Resource Booklet**. Make sure you look at all of the resources carefully before writing any answers.

Look again at the exam-style question on page 57 and the definition of 'select … and justify' below.

Pick one and name it in the space provided on the exam paper.

The list of three options in the question.

Select … and justify: Select one option from those given and justify your choice, using evidence from the resources provided and your own knowledge/understanding.

You must give reasons for choosing the option.

These reasons will include strengths and weaknesses and link evidence to how the option will solve the problem or issue.

Now look at these extracts from two students' responses to the exam-style question.

Isabel

Using mostly oil (option 1) for future oil suplies would be best because at the moment oil is used a lot around the world (figure 1) so it will be difficult to get rid of in the future. People need their cars and petrol is easy to get. The USA has oil supplies to last a very long time (figure 3). Wind energy is just not good enough and will not drive cars.

Haitham

There are big concerns about damage to the natural environment, especially greenhouse gas emissions from burning fossil fuels (Figure 2) which are causing climate change, and wind energy (option 2) offers a chance to reduce emissions from power stations as it is a clean source of energy. Despite renewables only making up 7.5% of the world's total energy consumption in 2014 (Figure 1), wind energy produces very cheap electricity which can lower costs for people and businesses.

(1) How well have Isabel and Haitham applied the definition of 'select … and justify' in their responses to the exam-style question? Tick ✓ the checkpoints that each student has met.

Checklist The student has...	Isabel	Haitham
• chosen and stated **one** of the options		
• used evidence to support their choice		
• included the strengths and weaknesses of the option		
• shown knowledge and understanding of the topic		
• used correct spelling, punctuation and grammar.		

(2) How could they be written more effectively to justify the geographical decision? Note ✎ your advice below.

a Isabel's response could ....

....

....

b Haitham's response could ....

....

....

1 How do I support my geographical decision with evidence?

Once you have chosen an option, you need to provide **evidence** from the resources and your own learning to show why it is the best. The resources provide evidence that can be used to support any of the three options as there is not a correct choice.

① Isabel decided that using oil is best. She looked for evidence in the resources and her studies to support this decision and noted down the **strengths** (or advantages) of oil.

Source of evidence	Evidence to support *Option 1: Use mostly oil*
Written statement or fact (Figure 3)	Oil was the second most important primary fuel consumed in the UK in 2016 (68 mtoe).
Information from a graph or map (Figure 1)	Oil is a flexible resource that can be used in vehicles, homes and industries.
Information from a photograph or sketch (Figure 5a)	Oil shale reserves provide 140 years supply.
Data (numbers or statistics) from a table, text, graph or map (Figure 4)	Oil consumption has increased by 33.33% in 25 years.
Use of views and opinions (Figure 2)	Non-conventional oil sources such as tar sands can be used.
Factual information from her studies beyond the resources provided.	Countries in Asia and North America need a lot of oil, especially from the Middle East which has over 800 billion barrels of reserves.

Draw ✐ a line linking her evidence to its source. One has been done for you.

② Now look for evidence in the resources (pages 65–66) that show the **strengths** (advantages) of using wind energy in the future (this is **Option 2**). Fill in ✐ the table below.

Source of evidence	Evidence to support Option 2: Use mostly wind energy
Written description of the changing importance of renewables in the world's energy consumption (Figure 1)	
Stating a reason for using wind energy in the future (Figure 2)	
Written statement or fact stating a reason for using wind energy in the future (Figure 3)	
Calculation: the percentage increase in the consumption of wind/solar/HEP energy between 2012 and 2016 (Figure 4)	
Information from a photograph: an advantage of using wind energy in the future (Figure 5b)	
Your studies – note **one** more strength (advantage) of using wind energy in the future	

2 How do I identify the strengths and weaknesses of the options?

Whichever option you choose, your answer must include a balance of the strengths (or advantages) and weaknesses (or disadvantages) of that option. You must also include some strengths and weaknesses of the other two options, and remember to support all of these with evidence from the resources.

(1) Look at Isabel's response below to the exam-style question on page 57.

> Option 1: Use mostly oil
>
> Using mostly oil for future energy supplies would be best because at the moment oil is about a third of the world's energy consumption (figure 1) so it will be difficult to get rid of this in the future. People depend a lot on their cars and so use a lot of petrol and oil and this type of transport will be needed in the next 30 years. It is a flexible resource and easy to transport which keeps costs low. People are used to using oil for energy and it will be difficult to change them. The USA could have oil supplies to last 140 years with huge reserves (figure 3).
>
> I think that oil is the best even though there can be problems with pollution and global warming. I don't think wind energy is good enough because it cannot supply enough energy even though it is free of pollution.

How well does Isabel justify her choice of Option 1: Use mostly oil?

a Circle (A) and label (✏) where she has stated the strengths (or advantages) of using mostly oil in the future.

b Highlight (✏) where she has included any weaknesses (or disadvantages) of using mostly oil in the future.

c Circle (A) and label (✏) where she has mentioned strengths (or advantages) of other options.

d Underline (A) where she has mentioned weaknesses of other options.

(2) Rewrite (✏) Isabel's response to improve any sections where strengths and weaknesses are missing or not clearly expressed. Check that your spelling, punctuation and grammar are correct.

....

....

....

....

....

....

....

3   **How do I write a justification of my geographical decision?**

When you write your justification, you are aiming to support your choice of option as well as to show why the other options are not suitable.

Look at the sentences below. They are all taken from different students' responses to the exam-style question, using **Option 2**: Use mostly wind energy.

Exam-style question

Select the option that you think would be best for meeting the energy needs of the world in the next 30 years. Justify your choice.

1 The USA can get more oil from Alaska and oil shale reserves (1 trillion barrels).

2 The USA is expanding its wind energy production, which currently supplies over 20 million homes with electricity.

3 Wind energy is only a small part of the world and UK energy consumption.

4 The wind is always available for turbines and is free, so that people and businesses can benefit from cheap electrical power in the future.

5 Oil is a flexible energy source as a liquid and can be used in cars and transported easily in bulk.

6 Wind power is one of the main renewable energy resources.

7 The world is experiencing climate change, and slowing this is important to protecting the natural environment.

1 In your first paragraph, you need to state the strengths of your choice, backed by evidence, and say how they will help solve the issue.

a Tick ✓ **three** sentences that you might use to build an effective first paragraph.

b In what order would you sequence your three chosen sentences?
Write 🖊 your order here. ☐ ☐ ☐

2 Now think about the sentences that are left. Why are they useful?

a Which sentence could you also use in support of the chosen option? (Another strength (advantage) of using mostly wind energy.) Label 🖊 it **S**.

b Which sentence identifies a weakness (disadvantage) in the chosen option? Label 🖊 it **W**.

c Which **two** sentences identify a strength (or advantage) for each of the other options? Label 🖊 them **A**.

3 Now put the sentences together. Write 🖊 a justification on paper for choosing **Option 2**: Use mostly wind energy. Add more strengths and weaknesses, backed by evidence from pages 65–66, if you can.

Sample response

To do well in the 'select and justify' decision-making question, you should:

- support your geographical decision with evidence
- identify and include the strengths and weaknesses of all the options
- write a detailed justification of your geographical decision.

Look again at this exam-style question and the resources on pages 65–66.

Look again at this exam-style question and the resources on pages 65–66.

Exam-style question

Select the option that you think would be best for meeting the energy needs of the world in the next 30 years. Justify your choice.

Then look at Haitham's response to it.

uses geographical terminology

uses evidence from the resources to support the strengths and weaknesses identified

identifies weaknesses of other option choices

identifies one or more strengths of other options

uses a sequence of paragraphs covering the structure of a justify answer

identifies strengths of the chosen option

links strengths and evidence to the question

identifies one or more weaknesses with the option choice

Chosen option: 2 Use mostly wind energy

Using wind energy, alongside other renewables, will be the best option for the next 30 years because it is a non-polluting energy source. There are great concerns about damage to the natural environment, especially greenhouse gas emissions which cause climate change, and wind energy offers the chance to reduce emissions from power stations. For example, in the USA, 12.3 gigatonnes of greenhouse gas emissions could be avoided with investment in wind energy.

Wind energy produces very cheap electricity which can lower total energy costs for people or businesses; this allows people to afford other things to improve their lives or businesses to make more profit.

There are some problems with wind energy. These include the fact that it is still a developing technology and may not play a major part in energy production until 2050 in big energy consuming countries such as the USA. In 2014, 'renewables' only accounted for 7.5% of the world's total energy consumption (Fig. 1).

Oil is a very important energy resource at the moment, accounting for about a third of the world's energy consumption in 2014 because it can be used in a variety of ways – from cars to heating to industries. It may take some time to change away from this because oil-using technologies are well established. However, oil will run out (Fig. 2) and so change must happen at some point in the future.

Identify all of the different things that Haitham has included in his answer by linking the annotations in the boxes to where he has included them in his response. (One is not done.)

Your turn!

You are now going to write your response to this exam-style question.

Exam-style question

Study the **three** options below for providing energy supplies over the next 30 years.

Option 1: Use mostly oil and other fossil fuels such as natural gas.

Option 2: Use mostly wind energy and other renewables such as solar power.

Option 3: Use a combination of oil and wind energy.

Select the option that you think would be best for meeting the energy needs of the world in the next 30 years. Justify your choice.

Use information from the Resource Booklet and knowledge and understanding from the rest of your geography course to support your answer. **(16 marks)**

(1) Study the resources on pages 65–66. Find evidence that you might use in your response to the exam-style question having chosen **Option 3**. Note (✐) down the evidence you will use in each paragraph of your response.

Paragraph 1	Main reason (strength) for selecting **Option 3**:
Paragraph 2	Another **two** reasons (strengths) for selecting **Option 3**:
Paragraph 3	The main weakness (disadvantage) of **Option 3**:
Paragraph 4	The main weaknesses (disadvantages) of **Options 1 and 2**:

(2) Now write (✐) your response to the above exam-style question on paper, using **Option 3** as your choice. Think about and check your spelling, punctuation, grammar and use of geographical terminology (worth 4 marks) as you create an effective response.

Review your skills

Check up

Review your response to the exam-style question on page 63. Tick ✓ the column to show how well you think you have done each of the following.

	Not quite ✓	Nearly there ✓	Got it! ✓
supported geographical decisions with evidence	☐	☐	☐
identified and included the strengths and weaknesses of all options in an answer	☐	☐	☐
written an effective response that justifies my geographical decision	☐	☐	☐

Look over all of your work in this unit. Note down ✐ the **three** most important things that you will need to remember when faced with 'select and justify' decision-making questions.

1 ....

2 ....

3 ....

Need more practice?

Plan ✐ your response to the exam-style question below, using the resources on pages 67–68.

Exam-style question

Study the **three** options below for how people living in the Solomon Islands should adapt to be ready for future challenges.

Option 1: Protect the coastal villages from flooding by the sea.

Option 2: Improve food and water security for people.

Option 3: Manage the natural coral reef and mangrove forest ecosystems.

Select the option that you think is the best for solving the challenges facing the people living in the Solomon Islands. Justify your choice.

Use information from the Resource Booklet (pages 67–68) and knowledge and understanding from the rest of your geography course to support your answer. (16 marks)

How confident do you feel about each of these **skills**? Colour ✐ in the bars.

1 How do I support my geographical decision with evidence?

2 How do I identify the strengths and weaknesses of the options?

3 How do I write a justification of my geographical decision?

Resource Booklet

For use with the exam-style question on page 57

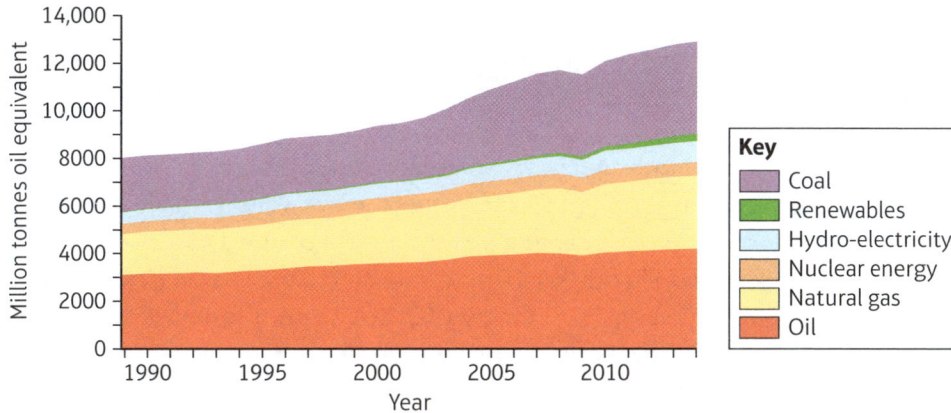

Figure 1 The world's energy consumption 1989–2014

Views of a big business using oil		Views of a major environmental group	
Benefits of oil	**Costs of wind energy**	**Costs of oil**	**Benefits of wind energy**
A flexible energy resource that can be used in vehicles, homes and industries	Views of landscape spoiled for local residents	Large amounts of air pollution are created, including CO_2	Clean energy source with no pollution once operational
Easy to transport in bulk in tankers or pipelines which keeps costs lower	Expensive transmission lines needed between offshore wind farms and cities needing electricity	It is a finite energy resource and so will run out at some point in the future	Large offshore windfarms generate large amounts of electricity for thousands of homes
Many established technologies available to use oil as an energy source	Turning turbine blades kill birds every year	Oil wells and refineries are large unsightly operations	Onshore wind farms can produce the cheapest electricity

Figure 2 Views of the costs and benefits of using oil and wind energy to meet future energy needs

For use with the exam-style question on page 57

The USA has enough oil to supply the country for about 30 years. The country is exploring alternative sources such as drilling in deep offshore areas (10 years supply), using oil from the area of the Arctic National Wildlife Refuge (ANWR) in Alaska or using oil shale reserves which could produce at least 1 trillion barrels of oil (140 years supply). However, the alternatives bring concerns about oil spills in the ocean, damaging important wildlife areas or polluting groundwater and causing ground movements through the fracking process.

In the USA, wind turbines are getting larger with some rotor blades over 100 metres in diameter and towers over 80 metres tall. Larger wind turbines mean more wind energy can be collected to generate very cheap electricity. The USA currently supplies wind power to over 20 million homes, and it is expanding fast in Texas and Illinois. Wind-power technology is still developing and more investment is needed. The industry currently employs 100,000 people in the USA; this is expected to increase to 600,000 by 2050. The USA aims to increase wind power supplies to 35% of the country's needs by 2050, which would also reduce greenhouse gas emissions by 12.3 gigatonnes.

Figure 3 Information about oil and wind energy in the USA

Year	TOTAL	Oil	Natural gas	Coal	Nuclear	Bioenergy & waste	Wind, solar, HEP
2012	208.1	67.0	73.3	40.9	15.2	8.4	2.3
2013	206.8	65.8	72.6	39.0	15.4	9.6	3.0
2014	194.0	66.0	66.1	31.5	13.9	11.2	3.6
2015	195.5	67.3	68.1	25.1	15.5	13.1	4.7
2016	192.8	68.0	76.7	12.4	15.4	14.2	4.6

Figure 4 UK energy consumption (million tonnes of oil equivalent)

Figure 5a Tar sand oil reserves, Alberta, Canada

Figure 5b Onshore windfarm

For use with the exam-style question on page 64

Selected villages	Coastal location on Choiseul Island	Land vulnerability rating	Community vulnerability rating	Coastal vulnerability rating	Marine vulnerability rating
Malivanga	NW	M	E	E	E
Ogho	NW	M	E	M	H
Varunga	NE	M	H	L	H
Panggoe	N	M	E	E	H
Susuka	N	H	H	E	H
Arariki-Kukutin	SE	L	E	E	E
Boeboe	SE	E	E	H	H
Papara	S	H	H	H	H
Panarui	S	H	E	H	H
Voza	SW	H	H	M	M

Table and key created by author. Data sourced from 'Ecosystem-based adaptation and climate change vulnerability - Choiseul Province, Solomon Islands', © SPREP SPC and GIZ 2013 and 'Choiseul Province Climate Change Vulnerability and Adaptation Assessment', Report Secretariat of the Pacific Community Cataloguing-in-publication data.

Key:

E Extreme = very high loss of livelihood and loss of ecosystem function from most impacts
H High = high loss of livelihood and ecosystem function from many impacts
M Moderate = some loss of livelihood and ecosystem function from some impacts
L Low = not likely to experience impacts in the short term
Land impacts = crop pests and diseases, flooding, landslides, soil erosion.
Community impacts = isolation, cultural change, population growth, food insecurity.
Coastal impacts = erosion, flooding, saltwater intrusion.
Marine impacts = mangrove and coral health, lower fish stocks.

Figure 6 Summary of Choiseul village vulnerability survey, Solomon Islands, 2014

In the Solomon Islands (South Pacific Ocean) most people live in coastal villages. Their lives are linked to the health of land and sea ecosystems. People make their living from natural resources such as timber and seaweed. They depend on ecosystems for fresh water and fertile soils, and healthy coral reefs for fishing and protection from climate change. However, the people are vulnerable due to a lack of development opportunities, a reliance on imported foods, a growing population and changes to the natural environment (such as 40 cm a year of coastal erosion, mangrove forest dieback and the effects of logging). The villagers have identified several adaptation options to help them meet the challenges ahead. Three of these options are:

1 **Coastal flood protection:** Plant vegetation buffers such as mangrove trees to help provide flood protection from rising sea levels, while at the same time improving the shoreline ecosystem. Also, relocate buildings and infrastructure to higher ground away from coastal flood zones.

2 **Food and water security:** Plant trees that provide valuable timber or crops and improve farming techniques. Also, protect river catchments and river ecosystems, build additional water storage and test water quality.

3 **Ecosystem management:** Manage the coral reef and mangrove forest ecosystems by controlling fishing, setting up fish nurseries and monitoring the use and condition of these ecosystems.

Figure 7 Information about the Solomon Islands

For use with the exam-style question on page 64

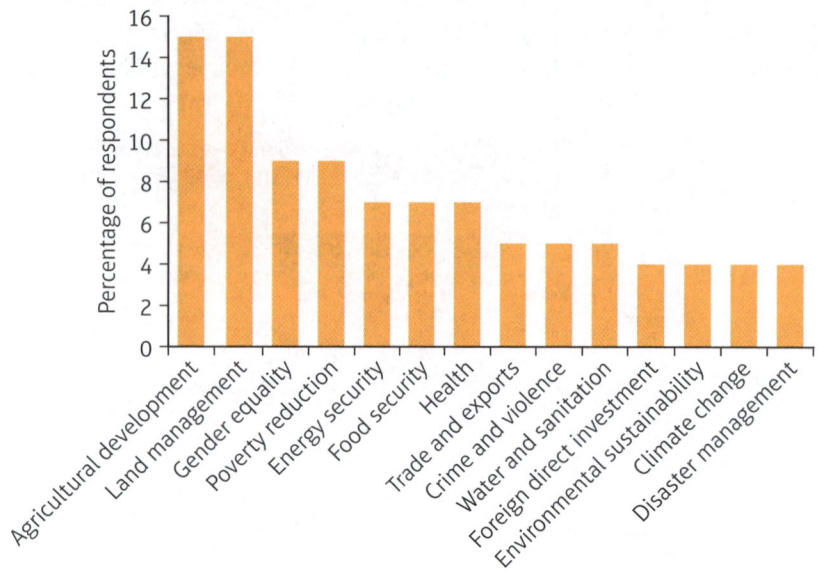

Figure 8 Results of a World Bank survey of development priorities in the Solomon Islands in 2015

Figure 9 A coastal village, Solomon Islands

Answers

Unit 1

Page 2

①

Title: what is the map about?	The world's biggest megacities in 2014
Key: in more detail, what does the map show?	The shading shows which countries are developed, emerging or developing. The largest megacities are also named and their populations shown.
Scale: how big is it?	The scale is 1 cm = 3000 km
Direction: which way is north?	North is towards the top of the map.

② The command words are *state*, *name* and *describe*.

③ i   37 million (Tokyo, Japan)

ii   Karachi, Pakistan

Page 3

①

a   **Yasmin** 2 out of 2 marks

Figure 2 shows the majority of the world's largest megacities are in emerging countries, especially in Asian countries like China. There are only three developed countries with large megacities – they are USA, South Korea and Japan. Pakistan is the only developing country with a megacity, Karachi, with 22 million people.

Sam 1 out of 2 marks

Most of the world's megacities are in emerging counties such as China. Tokyo, Japan, is the largest megacity with an amazing 37 million people.

b   For example:

- Yasmin makes effective points – she identifies a general pattern, then develops her points by giving some detail, as in her third point. However, there are 2 marks for the question so she doesn't really need to make three points.

- Sam's first point is useful, and he gives one short example. His second sentence doesn't really answer the question – it is more like an example.

②   For example:

Tokyo, Japan, is one of only three megacities in a developed country, but with 37 million people it has the largest population.

Page 4

①, **②** and **③**

The map shows that hurricanes form in the Atlantic and Pacific Oceans close to the Equator, because they need warm water to form. For example, many hurricanes start out in the Atlantic Ocean and travel westwards towards the Caribbean and Central America. Hurricanes are a hazard mainly affecting places between the Tropics of Cancer and Capricorn, but some reach the eastern parts of the USA.

Kate's phrase '*because they need warm water to form*' is correct, but she is beginning to explain the distribution of hurricanes.

④   Your response might include these points:

- Cyclones form in the Indian Ocean close to the Equator. South of the Equator they blow south-westwards then turn south.

- The places affected by cyclones are mainly between the Tropics of Cancer and Capricorn.

- Places affected by cyclones include North and West Australia, parts of South and South-east Asia, the coast of East Africa.

- An exception: parts of Western Australia affected by cyclones are outside the tropics.

Check you've described cyclones, not tornadoes or hurricanes.

Page 5

①   For example:

Point	Develop
South and east of the Tees–Exe line, the population density is higher than in the north and west.	For example, in southern England the population density is often over 500 people per km², particularly around London.

②   For example:

Pattern	Qualification	Exception
The population density in this half of the British Isles is generally lower.	In particular, much of Scotland and Wales has densities under 100 people per square kilometre.	However, there are exceptions. For example, urban areas of central Scotland and south Wales.

Page 6

①   **a**   Yasmin – PD; Sam – PQE

b   **Yasmin:** *In Birmingham, inner-city wards like Washwood Heath, Aston, Ladywood and Sparkbrook have most benefit claimants as shown on the key. Away from the city centre, in the suburbs towards the top of the map, there are many less claimants. These areas are shaded yellow.*

Sam: *Overall, the inner-city wards have the highest number of claimants. For example Ladypool and Aston both have 336–500 claimants. Further away from the centre, most wards have fewer claimants, especially in the north of Birmingham where nearly everywhere has 15–100 claimants. There are some exceptions. There are higher numbers of benefit claimants on the south edge of the city and right in the city centre where fewer people...*

c   For example:

- Yasmin only makes two points. Her first point is correct and includes some examples from the map. Her second point could be improved with geographical language (e.g. 'north') and by including figures.

- Sam starts by describing the general pattern then makes two detailed points, including places and accurate figures from the map. The start of his third point is also accurate, but he doesn't finish it.

Page 7

① Washwood Heath or Sparkbrook

② Describe the distribution of residents with no qualifications in Birmingham.

For example, circle the entries in the Key with the highest and the lowest percentage of residents with no qualifications; circle these regions on the map; circle clusters of other percentages; circle exceptions (anomalies).

③ and **④**. Some of the points you might make:

- Overall, inner-city wards north and east of Birmingham city centre have the highest percentage of people with no qualifications – examples are Washwood Heath and Sparkbrook with over 35.8%, and Aston with 30.5–35.8%.

- The outer city wards on the south edge of the city have medium to high numbers of people with no qualifications, with 25–35.8%.

- Overall, there isn't a clear pattern of wards where many people have no qualifications – inner-city wards in the north and east have the highest concentrations of people with no qualifications, but in the south of the city a number of outer-city wards have quite high levels.

- This means there are some exceptions: the inner wards just south and west of the city centre have very few people with no qualifications, in contrast to those north and east of the city centre. East of the city centre, inner and outer city wards have many people with no qualifications, including the wards east of Washwood Heath.

Unit 2

Page 10

① For example:

- Major road A548 may get flooded
- Near major river

② **a** and **b** For example:

The area is protected from the river by an embankment, therefore it is likely flooding has happened in the past or could be a risk in future. The area includes an industrial estate and a major road, so if flooding occurs there is a risk of lots of damage and disruption.

Page 11

② 3.25 km

③ **a** 4.5 cm

b 1.1 km

④ **a** 8 cm

b 4 km

Page 12

①

		✓ or ✗	Correction	
The golf course south of the River Dee	3965	✓		The student read these the wrong way round
Chester city centre, around the cathedral	6640	✗	4066	
The suburb of Handbridge south of the city centre	4065	✗	4165	The student read across to grid line 40 instead of 41

②

		✓ or ✗	Correction	
Chester railway station	415670	✗	413670	415 wasn't quite accurate enough
Chester cathedral	406665	✓		
The Club House on Chester golf course	393659	✗	395659	The student found the grid reference for the golf course symbol, not the Club House

Page 13

① **a** ☐ i Mostly flat with some gentle slopes

☐ ii Very steeply sloping

☒ iii Both steep and very steep slopes

☐ iv Gently sloping

b Other spot heights on the map extracts: 216 m or 154 m

c
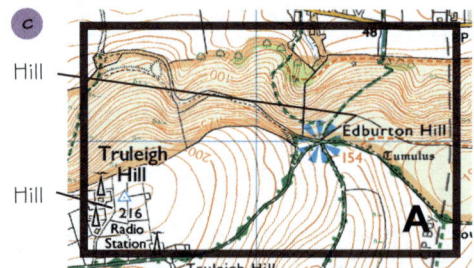

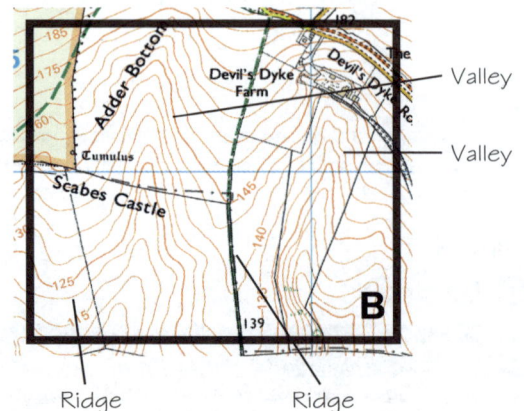

Page 14

① **a** Jade   Abid

     i   Industrial estate ✓   Farmland ✗

    ii   1.4 km ✗   1.75 km ✓

b   **Jade:** Jade has measured the straight-line distance, not the distance by road. Always check the question carefully!

     Abid: Abid may be looking at the wrong grid square – farmland is the main land use in 3766. So it's worth double-checking grid references.

② **a** and **b**

There is an embankment in 3865 so flooding is obviously a risk nearby. The land here has no contours – it is flat and at risk of flooding and as a result floodwater could move quickly across a large area, causing damage. ~~There are also a number of small streams in the area and nearby farmland.~~

c   Abid uses map evidence to make two points, each linked with accurate development text, matching the 2 marks for this question. However, he doesn't need a third point, which is also not really focused.

Page 15

①   C   Ridge with steep slopes

②   2.5 km

③   For example:

- Beach symbol seems to be sandy near the town
- Map evidence shows Swanage is a tourist town; groynes stop beach sand being washed away.
- Groynes along the town section of the beach, not along the cliffs to the north.

④   For example:

Point	Develop
The sea defences in 0379 are groynes.	They were built because otherwise longshore drift would wash the sandy beach away.
The groynes are along the beach nearest the town.	Map evidence shows this is a tourist town, so the beach is an important attraction.

Unit 3

Page 18

①   sloping valley sides – left

     meandering river – centre

     flat flood plain – foreground, centre

     wooded slope – right

② **a**   X is a river cliff

b   For example:

     River cliffs are steep slopes formed by erosion on the outside of a meander bend.

c   As well as the river cliff, you should be able to identify and label a meander, slip-off slope and flood plain. You might have also identified a meander neck and point bar.

Page 19

①   I'll describe how the meanders form. Firstly, wide bends form where the river valley is wider and flatter, like the Severn valley in Shropshire in Figure 2. Secondly, lateral erosion happens on the outside of a bend …

②   For example:

I'll describe how the meanders form. Firstly, wide river bends form on flood plains in the middle and lower course of rivers where the valley is wider and flatter, like the Severn valley in Shropshire in Figure 2. Secondly, on the outside of a bend the river's velocity is high and has more energy for lateral erosion. Here the river undercuts the banks, which then become steeper and steeper, forming river cliffs. In addition, deposition happens on the inside of bends where the velocity and energy of the river is less, forming a gently sloping bank called a slip-off slope, and a curved point bar.

Page 20

①   **a** , **b** and **c**

Nathan

The River Severn winds lazily through fertile farmland in its broad, verdant valley. Its sinuous bends (or meanders) are the result of complex geographical processes which leave sediments on the flat land each side of the river.

Amandeep   course   erodes   flood plain

Meanders like those on the River Severn form in the middle and lower part of a river where the valley is wide and flat. The river wears away at the outside of bends, where the water is faster. It forms steeper banks and the bends get larger and closer to each other. Eventually, only a small piece of land separates these twisty bends which are called meanders.

     meander neck   the velocity is greater

②   For example, Nathan's main problem is he's overdone writing adjectives, and not focused on describing the processes. Next time he should describe each stage in how a meander forms, making sure to include more geographical language.

③   3 minutes

Page 21

①   The formation of a bar results from a process that moves sediment along the coast. This starts with the wind causing the swash to move the sediment up the beach at an angle. Due to gravity, the backwash brings the wave down the beach. This transports the beach sediment along the coast, consequently when it comes to the mouth of a bay, this forms a spit which sticks out from the coast.

②   For example:

- Nathan didn't finish explaining the process of how a bar forms. He needs to explain how a spit grows to join the land on the other side of the bay to become a bar with a lagoon behind it.
- Including how the prevailing wind causes longshore drift would show he really understands the process, and help link his second and third sentences into an effective explanation.

Page 22

(1) I am going to describe how the bar in Figure 1 was formed. A long time ago longshore drift moved sediments like sand and pebbles along the coastline away from the prevailing wind. Then at a bay or river mouth, the transported material was deposited offshore. Next a spit forms, stretching across the bay. When the spit reaches land on the far side of the bay, a lagoon forms because streams can't reach the sea.

(2) For example:

- The question asks for an explanation, but Amandeep starts off by saying she will describe the process.

- The middle part is correct, but she could perhaps improve on her explanation here. For example, 'the transported sediments are deposited offshore due to wave action – so over time this develops into a spit, which grows across the bay or river mouth'.

- Her last sentence focuses on the lagoon, rather than explaining how a spit becomes a bar.

(3) **a** Her response would be awarded 2–3 marks.

b For example:

	Amandeep
Uses the photograph, caption, command word and mark to guide her response	Amandeep's response shows that she used the photograph and mark to guide her writing, but she got into a muddle with the command word.
Includes the ingredients for a good explanation	Amandeep has: • started with a short statement to help focus on the photo and landform • tried to make the same number of points as marks, although not all her points are well developed • included plenty of geographical language about landforms and processes.
Focuses on explaining, not describing	Amandeep has described as well as explained. Using more cause-and-effect conjunctions would help her focus better on explaining why the process happens.

Page 23

(1) **i** C a lagoon

ii Some points you might make:

- An initial statement showing you know that landform Y is a bar, perhaps adding it is a landform of deposition on the south Devon coast.

- The first processes are wave action and longshore drift, so wave energy erodes and transports sediments along the coast, away from the prevailing wind.

- Explain how a break in the coast, such as a river mouth or bay, leads to the deposition of these materials just offshore, in deeper water.

- Explain how this material gradually builds up – deposition extends the beach across the river mouth or bay to form a spit.

- Sometimes continued deposition may cause the spit to grow right across the bay to form a bar. You might explain that bars will only form across smaller river mouths where more material is deposited by wave action than the river can erode.

(2) Student's own answers

(3) Student's own answer

Unit 4

Page 26

(1) **a** The graph shows a scatter graph of people with access to clean water and child deaths in 12 countries.

b The x-axis shows access to clean water in percent (%).

c The y-axis shows child deaths per thousand.

(2) Command word: Label

Marks: 2 marks

(3)

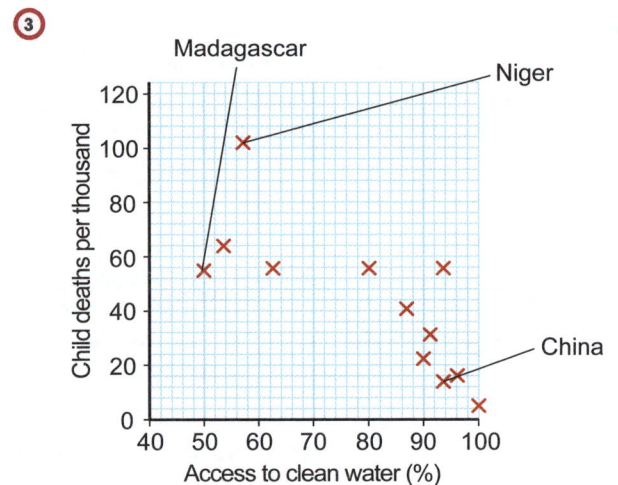

Page 27

(1)

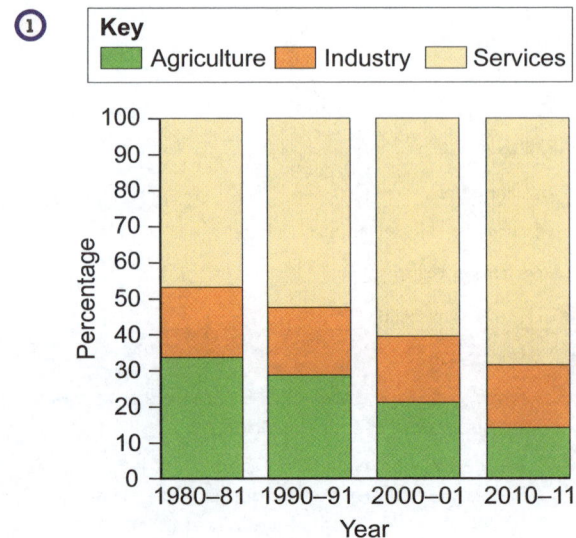

(2)

GDP by sector	Agriculture	Industry	Services
2010–11	13%	17%	70%

Page 28

(1) i   C 300 $US billion

     ii   2006

(2) **a** and **b**

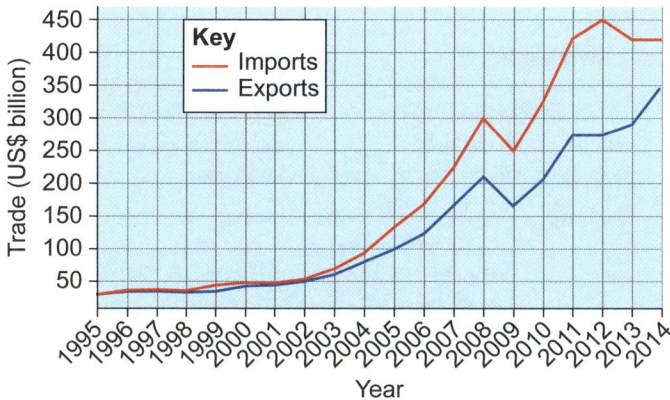

(3) For example:

- From 1995 to 2003, India's imports *increased slowly*.
- India's imports *increased rapidly* from 2003 to 2008.
- From 2008 to 2009, India's imports *dropped* from $300 billion to $250 billion.
- They *peaked* in 2012, reaching $450 billion, then *fell slightly*.

Page 29

(1) As GDP increases, life expectancy increases.

(2)

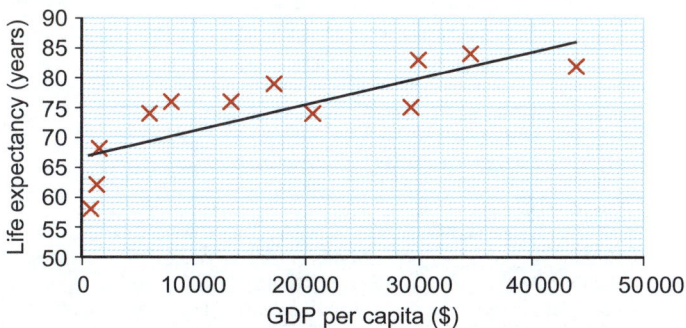

(3) **a**   Positive correlation

     b   The scatter graph shows that as GDP per capita increases, so does life expectancy – this is a positive correlation. The countries with the highest GDP, over about $25 000 per person, have generally high life expectancy. This may be because wealthier countries can spend more money on healthcare. The poorest countries with lower life expectancy may also have greater risk of disease. There are some exceptions – for example, one country has a GDP of nearly $30 000 per capita, but life expectancy of only 75 years.

Page 30

(1) ii   Figure 2 and the line of best fit show a ==negative relationship between access to clean water and child deaths.== This means that as one goes up so does the other, meaning ==as countries get cleaner water, fewer children die. For example, the country with 100% clean water has child deaths of about 5%.== Mainly the poorer countries have higher child deaths.

(2) **a**   Sunita's line of best fit does not go through all the data points, with the same number on each side.

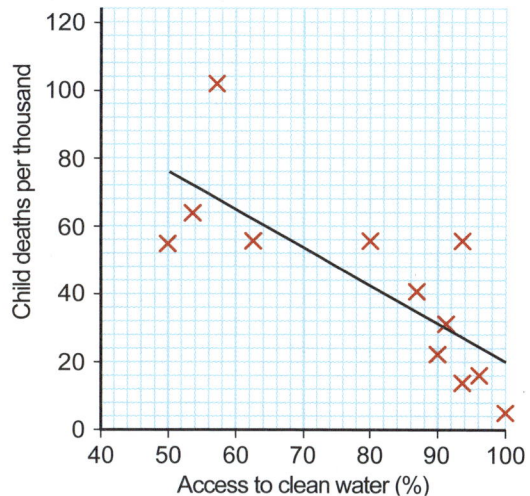

     b   Figure 2 and the line of best fit show a negative relationship between access to clean water and child deaths in these countries. So, as access to clean water increases, fewer children die. For example, the country with 100% clean water has child deaths of about 5 per thousand. There is a group of four countries where under 70% have clean water, and child deaths are over 50 per thousand.

Page 31

(1) For part i, Cameroon correctly plotted at x-axis 75, y-axis 55; Algeria correctly plotted at x-axis 85, y-axis 75. Look back at page 26 *Get started* and follow the instructions to read/plot data points to help you.

For part ii, check you draw your line of best fit with roughly the same number of points on each side of the line.

(2) For part iii, you might make these points:

- Countries with good access to clean water have longer life expectancy than those with poor access to clean water; as access to clean water improves, overall so does life expectancy.
- The scatter graph with its line of best fit shows there is a positive correlation/relationship between access to clean water and life expectancy.
- You could add details – for example, most countries with over 85% clean water have life expectancy over 70 years.
- There are some exceptions – for example, there are two counties with over 85% clean water but life expectancy under 70 years. The country with only 50% access to clean water doesn't have the lowest life expectancy.

(3) Student's own answer

Unit 5

Page 34

① 282 m³/s

Range: 282 − 167 = 115 m³/s

② **a** 167 cumecs (the lowest peak discharge)

This is the lowest of all the river discharges shown, so the amount of water in the river is much less than previous years.

b 94 cumecs (the range)

The range allows you to compare the highest and lowest values over several years. It does not help to explain why 2014–15 was a difficult year for farmers in Teesdale.

Page 35

① percentage change = $\dfrac{\text{actual change}}{\text{original amount}}$ × 100

actual change = 2015 value − 2006 value

= 1.69 − 1.27 = 0.42 million

percentage change = $\dfrac{0.42}{1.27}$ × 100

= +33.07% (to 2 d.p.)

② Mushin : Shomolu

1.76 : 1.36

÷ 1.76   ÷ 1.76

1 : $\dfrac{1.36}{1.76}$ = 0.7727…

Ratio is 1 : 0.77 (to 2 d.p.)

Page 36

① Median: 1.36 million (Isabel's answer is correct)

Inter-quartile range:

1.91 **1.76** 1.69 **1.36** 1.14 **0.84** 0.69

upper quartile − lower quartile = 1.76 − 0.84 = 0.92 million

Isabel has incorrectly calculated the inter-quartile range. The figure 1.22 million represents the range in the whole data set (that is the highest number minus the lowest number). The correct answer is 0.92 million.

② Pebble data: 14 **11 10** 8 7 **6 5** 3

Upper quartile: $\dfrac{11 + 10}{2}$ = 10.5 mm

Lower quartile: $\dfrac{6 + 5}{2}$ = 5.5 mm

Inter-quartile range: 10.5 − 5.5 = 5 mm

Page 37

① The River Tees has a peak discharge over 10 times greater than the River Gipping. The inter-quartile range also shows that the River Tees has a greater variation in peak discharges. These differences could be due to the rock type. The River Gipping could have more permeable rock so that any rainfall soaks away while in the River Tees area it runs off the surface into the river. The discharges could also be different because the River Tees area has much higher precipitation than the Gipping area.

② Factors leading to unreliable data: Equipment failure or inaccuracy; Data collected over a short time period; Small sample size; Estimated data

Page 38

① Data: 1203 **1109** 1065 **857** 718 **529** 435

i Median = 857 tonnes/day (Annabel is incorrect; Grahame is correct)

ii Inter-quartile range = 1109 − 529 = 580 tonnes/day (both student answers are correct)

② **a** , **b** and **c**

Annabel

It will be higher because the population of Mushin has grown by a third, so more people means that more waste will be created.

Grahame

It's higher because people have become wealthier and so buy more products and everything has more packaging.

d Annabel has explained that more waste is generated due to an increase in the population. She has used data (an increase of a third since 2006) to support her explanation, whereas Grahame has not.

Page 39

① percentage change = $\dfrac{\text{actual change}}{\text{original amount}}$ × 100

actual change = 2015 value − 2006 value

= 1.76 − 1.32 = 0.44 million

percentage change = $\dfrac{0.44}{1.32}$ × 100

= +33.33% (to 2 d.p.)

② Ajeromi-Ifelodun : Apapa

1.44 : 0.52

÷ 1.44   ÷ 1.44

1 : $\dfrac{0.52}{1.44}$ = 0.3611…

Ratio is 1 : 0.36 (to 2 d.p.)

③ Reasons could include:

- difficult to get rid of solid waste because so much is created by lots of people and is left lying around
- not enough clean water for everyone
- not enough proper housing for everyone
- difficult to supply a sanitation system for all houses so little treatment of sewage.

Page 40

Instruction or command	What it tells you to do
Calculate the range …	Highest value minus lowest value
Calculate the ratio of ….	Divide the lower value being compared by the higher value. Write the answer in the form 1 : *n*, where the higher value = 1.
Calculate the percentage increase/ decrease …	$\dfrac{\text{actual change}}{\text{original amount}}$ × 100
Suggest **two** reasons …	Give explanations for geographical patterns within data.
Calculate the inter-quartile range …	Middle value of the top half of the data minus middle value of the lower half of the data
Find the median …	The middle value in a list of numbers placed in numerical order

Unit 6

Page 42

1 The following elements should be ticked:

- He has clearly introduced his megacity. *(Mumbai is clearly located and a fact given about its size.)*
- The megacity is in a developing or emerging country. *(Mumbai is in India, which is an emerging country.)*
- He has identified several factors which affect the quality of life in his named megacity. *(He mentions the fact that the housing is rent-controlled, high levels of corruption, the government being inefficient and lack of sanitation and waste disposal.)*
- He has explained why these factors affect the quality of life in his megacity. *(He could be more explicit about how some of the factors affect the quality of life but he does explain the impact of the inefficient government well and links this to poor waste disposal.)*
- He has identified which of the factors is the most important. *(Lack of adequate waste disposal and sanitation is identified as the most important factor.)*
- He has used data to illustrate these factors. *(His answer could probably be improved with the addition of more data. However, he does give figures for the number of people sharing a latrine in Dharavi to illustrate his point about poor sanitation.)*
- He has used geographical language and connectives to make good points. *(He has used both throughout, which means he has been able to develop most of his points effectively.)*
- He has explained why he thinks this factor is the most important. *(He begins to explain this in the final sentence.)*

2 For example:

Chris's response is fairly effective. It has all of the ingredients of a good answer – all of the points above are ticked – and some of these, such as his conclusion, work well. There are a couple of areas, for example, explaining how the factors affect quality of life and supporting his points with data, which could be more developed.

Page 43

1 For example:

- levels of air and water pollution
- levels of transport congestion
- access to education
- crime levels

2 For example, from most (1) to least (5) significant:

1. Adequate sanitation and waste disposal can dramatically improve people's quality of life.
2. The majority of employment is in in the 'informal sector', which means that working conditions are poor.
3. The government is inefficient and bureaucratic so it takes a long time for improvements to happen.

4. A rapid rise in private cars means that Mumbai's roads are frequently gridlocked, leading to 'super dense' traffic congestions.
5. Mumbai is a relatively wealthy megacity which has high levels of foreign direct investment.

3 For example:

The high levels of traffic congestion make it difficult for people to travel to work but it also increases the levels of air pollution. This air pollution can be very bad for people's health and cause breathing difficulties. Access to education is important if people are to get well-paid jobs in the formal sector and avoid a life of crime.

Page 44

1 1 B, 2 A, 3 D, 4 C

2 For example:

While 100% of Cairo's population has access to water and 97% have access to sanitation, the water supply is not continuous. Around 40% of the population do not get water for more than 3 hours per day and three large districts do not receive any piped water. The water supply is often poor quality and, consequently, it is estimated that each year over 17,000 children die from diarrhoea.

Page 45

1 For example:

Factor	Evidence
Access to education	Enrolment in Cairo's secondary schools is about 89% although attendance is focused in wealthier areas and 54% of those in poorer areas do not attend school regularly.
Traffic congestion	The World Bank found that the annual cost of traffic congestion in Cairo was around 4% of Egypt's GDP. Many wealthy school children who commute to New Cairo's private schools can expect to spend over 3 hours per day in a car.
Air pollution	Known in Egypt as 'the black cloud', dense smog annually covers Cairo and the Nile delta and has done since 1997. This cloud accounts for 42% of the country's air pollution and is caused by local farmers burning rice straw.

2 For example:

I think that access to education is the most important factor as not only can it lead to more profitable job opportunities in the formal sector, but female literacy is also strongly linked to fertility. Both these things mean that education is likely to lead to more disposable income and an increased quality of life.

3 **a** *Lack of adequate sanitation and waste disposal is probably the most important factor affecting quality of life* **(iii)** *because if the water supply is highly polluted, this can cause diseases* **(i)**, *such as cholera, which can be fatal and trap people into a cycle of poverty* **(ii)**.

b For example, he could explain the cycle of poverty a little more clearly as this is the first time he mentions this idea. He could also suggest why other factors, such as an inefficient government, are less important.

Page 46

1 **a**, **b** and **c**.

Coastal flooding is when low-lying land which is normally dry is flooded with seawater. There are several physical reasons why this can happen. Strong winds can push the water onto the coastline to create a storm surge. This often happens during hurricanes or cyclones. Global warming can also cause sea levels to rise which can flood low-lying land.

However, human activity is also important. In some places people have re-claimed land from the sea and it is often found below sea-level. Also, humans have changed the processes in other places along the coast by putting in hard and soft engineering. This can protect some parts of the coast but move the problem of erosion and flooding somewhere else. So, if groynes are put in somewhere to keep the beach in place there won't be a large beach down the coast, and this means the waves can get to the land more easily and flood it. People also build houses on the coast for a good sea view. If they didn't build it wouldn't matter so much if the land flooded but because they do, it can be very expensive if the coast does flood.

In conclusion, I think that at the moment the causes of coastal flooding are mainly a result of human activity because they have made it more likely to cause damage. But in the future, if global warming increases and hurricanes happen more often, then I think that physical factors may be more important.

d ✓

2 For example:

1 Explain more clearly what you mean by 'human factors have made it more likely to cause damage'.

2 Explain why you think physical factors may be more important than human factors if global warming occurs.

Page 47

1 For example:

Human factors

- Settlements – people who live near the coast are at risk of flooding.

- Tourism – in many coastal towns tourism is very important for the local economy.

- Agriculture – sea level rise and coastal flooding has already led to the loss of coastal farmland which can affect the local economy.

Physical factors

- Sea level rise – link to anthropogenic (human caused) global warming.

- Storm surges – large-scale increase in sea level due to storms.

2 For example:

Human

- Settlements – over 20 million people in the UK live near the coast.

- Tourism – 13% of jobs in Dawlish are in tourism.

- Agriculture – agricultural land is of low value; the fishing industry in the Exe estuary, Devon is likely to be affected by coastal flooding.

Physical

- Sea level rise – sea level along the English Channel has risen by about 12 cm in the last 100 years and is likely to rise by the same amount by 2030.

- Storm surges – can raise sea levels by 3 metres.

3 Coastal flooding is mainly a result of physical factors but human factors can increase the risk and impact.

4 Student's own answer

Unit 7

Page 50

1 **a** I need to weigh up the relative success of the different responses to earthquakes in a named developed country. I will need facts and figures from my case study so that I can measure the various responses.

b I will need to identify the strengths and weaknesses of the response to an earthquake in a developed country case study that I have studied. Using this, I will then need to make a decision about whether the strengths are greater than the weaknesses overall.

2 **a**

Checklist I have …	
correctly identified what needs to be evaluated	✓
identified how I will go about measuring the value or success of this	✓
suggested there may be alternatives/ improvements	✓
identified how I will draw this together in my conclusion	✓
named a developed country.	✓

b Salma named a developed country and suggested that there may be alternatives or improvements which I didn't include in my answer. I need to make sure I include these features so that I have evaluated effectively.

Page 51

1

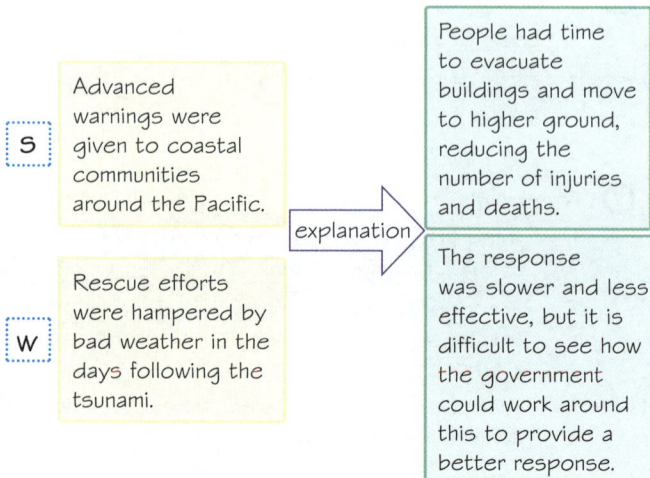

S | Advanced warnings were given to coastal communities around the Pacific.

W | Rescue efforts were hampered by bad weather in the days following the tsunami.

explanation →

People had time to evacuate buildings and move to higher ground, reducing the number of injuries and deaths.

The response was slower and less effective, but it is difficult to see how the government could work around this to provide a better response.

2 a Examples of strengths:

- Rescue workers were mobilised to deal with the earthquake crisis – Australia, China, India, New Zealand, South Korea and the USA sent search and rescue teams.

- Good preparation – school students and workers take part in annual National Disaster Prevention Day on 1 September.

Examples of weaknesses:

- Displacement and temporary shelters – more than 130,000 people were displaced and had to live in temporary shelters where food and supplies were severely limited.

- Power supply – it took several weeks to restore the power supply.

b
- Rescue workers – well-trained and co-ordinated rescue workers reduced the number of injuries and fatalities.

- Good preparation – as earthquakes cannot be predicted the most effective long-term response is to be prepared.

- Displacement and temporary shelters – disease can easily spread in poor and confined spaces.

- Power supply – this reduced the region's manufacturing and business output in the short term.

Page 52

1 a and **b**.

Statement	Strength or weakness?	Score (10–1)
Advanced warnings were given to coastal communities around the Pacific by the Pacific Tsunami Warning Center.	S	9
The Japanese government requested international aid from Australia, China, India, New Zealand and South Korea.	S	7
There was disruption to roads and communications which made it difficult to get food to the people who needed it.	W	6
140,000 people were evacuated from the Fukushima power plant.	S	9
Tens of thousands of prefabricated temporary houses were set up in Sendai.	S	3
The Red Cross and Red Crescent provided support to the government along with private companies and NGOs.	S	7
Rescue efforts were hampered by bad weather in the days following the tsunami.	W	6

2 a Strengths: 35
a Weaknesses: 12

3 The 'strengths' side has the highest score – 35 against 12. Consequently, it seems that the response to the Japanese earthquake was relatively strong and effective.

Page 53

1 a, **b** and **c**. For example:

In conclusion, the response to the Japanese earthquake was a success/failure. The government, private companies and NGOs responded quickly and effectively/slowly and ineffectively and there were many/few weaknesses in their response.

- One weakness was that it took several weeks for the power supply to be brought online which reduced the region's manufacturing and business output in the short term.

- This could be improved by employing more electricians to get the power supply online more quickly.

2 a, **b** and **c**. For example:

In conclusion, I think that the response to the Japanese earthquake was more effective than the response to the Haiti earthquake. The Japanese were prepared and had early warning systems but the Haitians are poor and were unprepared. Many people were trapped in buildings and it was difficult to rescue them because no one was in charge. The response to the Haiti earthquake would have been more effective if they had responded in a similar way to the Japanese. Retrofitting 'earthquake proof' technology would have stopped buildings from falling down and killing people.

Page 54

1 a, **b** and **c**.

The conclusion to my fieldwork in Birmingham was that the quality of life in Sparkbrook ward was not as high as the quality of life in Ladywood ward. This is likely to be accurate as the secondary data from the census supported the observations that I made as I walked around the two areas. However, the sampling strategy that I used may have made the conclusion less reliable. I only did my environmental quality survey in three places and I might have missed other places that would have given me different results and a different conclusion. I also carried out my questionnaires at 2 pm on a Tuesday afternoon and it was raining. Therefore, there were lots of people I couldn't ask, for example school children who were probably in school, and some of the people who I did ask were rude and didn't want to answer because they didn't want to get wet. On balance, I think that my conclusion is fairly reliable. If I was going to do my fieldwork again I would make sure that I did my environmental quality survey in more places and I would also make sure that I did my questionnaires at different times so that I would get a more representative sample.

2 For example:

Sasha's response is good because she identifies that her results are supported by secondary data, but is clear about the weaknesses of the data and gives examples to support her points. I also like the way that she suggests improvements to her fieldwork.

One way she could improve her response is by adding a bit of detail to the strength of her fieldwork. She only has one – and it's a really important one – but she could give some examples of her results and those in the secondary data so it's clear just how it supported her observations.

Page 55

① and **②**

Score	Strengths/Weaknesses	Explanations
9	• Similar results to those from the census (strength)	• Two pieces of data from two different sources reach the same conclusion.
7	• Several methods used (strength)	• Gives different views about the same thing rather than just using one method which only provides one perspective.
3	• Sampling (weakness / strength)	• This is a weakness as it would be much better to sample the whole population, but this is impossible. So, it is also a strength because I used a sampling strategy rather than just choosing people and places at random.

③ Strengths – 16; Weaknesses – 3

④ The strengths are greater than the weaknesses and therefore this suggests that on balance my fieldwork conclusion is fairly reliable.

I could have used more sampling points as I only spoke to 20 people and visited three places. My conclusion would have been more reliable if I had spoken to more people and if they had been more representative of the total population.

⑤ Student's own answer

Unit 8

Page 58

①

Checklist The student has...	Isabel	Haitham
• chosen and stated **one** of the options	✓	✓
• used evidence to support their choice	✓	✓
• included the strengths and weaknesses of the option		✓
• shown knowledge and understanding of the topic		✓
• used correct spelling, punctuation and grammar.		✓

② *Isabel's response could be more effective if she used precise data from the resources rather than making general statements. For example, 'The USA currently has oil supplies to last another 30 years and the potential to drill for supplies that will last for 140 years.' She needs to recognise weaknesses of using oil. She could also use data to say why wind energy is not a suitable alternative.*

Haitham's response could be more effective if he began by stating his chosen option and then provided evidence to support his choice before saying why one of the other options was not suitable. Perhaps more evidence could have been included.

Page 59

①

Source of evidence	Evidence to support *Option 1: Use mostly oil*
Written statement or fact (Figure 3)	*Oil shale reserves provide 140 years supply.*
Information from a graph or map (Figure 1)	*Oil consumption has increased by 33.33% in 25 years.*
Information from a photograph or sketch (Figure 5a)	*Non-conventional oil sources such as tar sands can be used.*
Data (numbers or statistics) from a table, text, graph or map (Figure 4)	*Oil was the second most important primary fuel consumed in the UK in 2016 (68 mtoe).*
Use of views and opinions (Figure 2)	*Oil is a flexible resource that can be used in vehicles, homes and industries.*
Factual information from her studies beyond the resources provided	*Countries in Asia and North America need a lot of oil, especially from the Middle East which has over 800 billion barrels of reserves.*

②

Source of evidence	Examples of evidence to support Option 2: Use mostly wind energy
Written description of the changing importance of renewables in the world's energy consumption (Figure 1)	*Since 2000 the amount of renewable energy consumed has increased significantly.*
Stating a reason for using wind energy in the future (Figure 2)	*Wind energy is a clean energy source and can help reduce pollution.*
Written statement or fact stating a reason for using wind energy in the future (Figure 3)	*Wind turbine technology is improving all the time and is able to generate more energy, such as being larger (80 metres high and 100 metres wide) to catch more wind.*
Calculation: the percentage increase in the consumption of wind/solar/HEP energy between 2012 and 2016 (Figure 4)	*percentage change* $= \dfrac{actual\ change}{original\ amount} \times 100$ *2012 = 2.3 mtoe, 2016 = 4.6 mtoe* $= 4.6 - 2.3 = 2.3$ $= \dfrac{2.3}{2.3} \times 100 = 100\%$
Information from a photograph: an advantage of using wind energy in the future (Figure 5b)	*Wind energy is suitable for onshore areas, especially at higher altitudes.*
Your studies – note **one** more strength (advantage) of using wind energy in the future	*People are more aware of their carbon footprint now and this has helped increase the wind-generating capacity to 3% of global energy production.*

Page 60

① ⓐ – ⓓ

Option 1: Use mostly oil

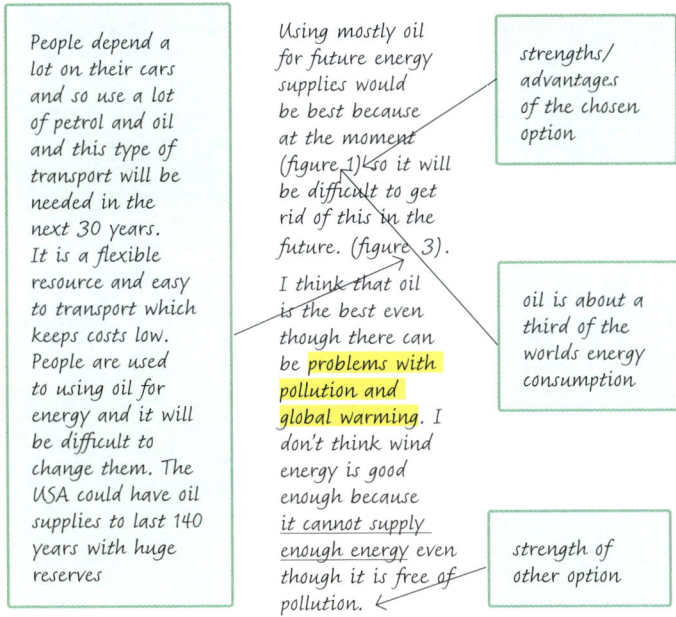

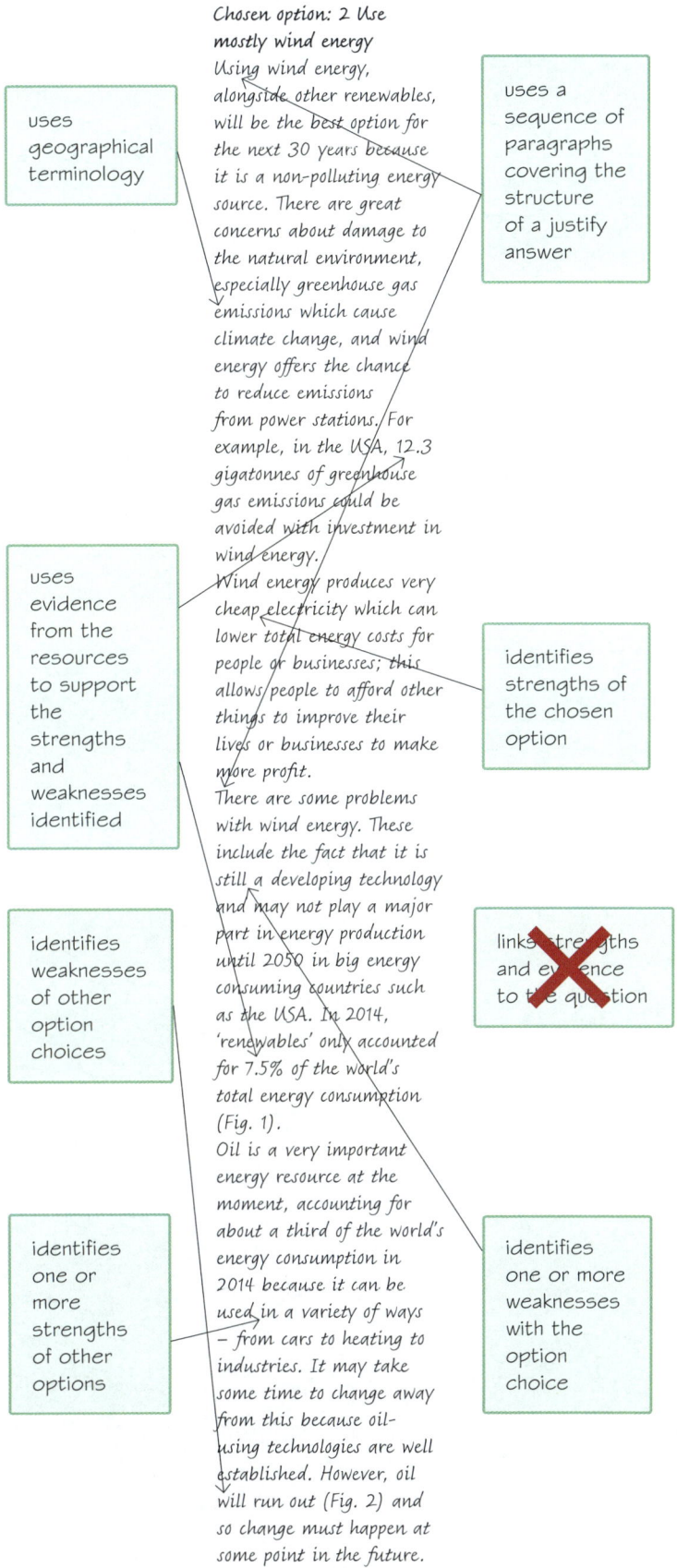

People depend a lot on their cars and so use a lot of petrol and oil and this type of transport will be needed in the next 30 years. It is a flexible resource and easy to transport which keeps costs low. People are used to using oil for energy and it will be difficult to change them. The USA could have oil supplies to last 140 years with huge reserves

Using mostly oil for future energy supplies would be best because at the moment (figure 1) so it will be difficult to get rid of this in the future. (figure 3).
I think that oil is the best even though there can be problems with pollution and global warming. I don't think wind energy is good enough because it cannot supply enough energy even though it is free of pollution.

strengths/ advantages of the chosen option

oil is about a third of the worlds energy consumption

strength of other option

② For example:

Using mostly oil for future energy supplies would be best because at the moment oil is the largest source of energy with 4000 mtoe consumed in 2014 (Figure 1), so it will be difficult to replace this quickly in 30 years. People depend a lot on machinery and transport that uses oil or its refined products (e.g. cars), and while some countries are planning to ban petrol and diesel cars soon (e.g. UK) this type of transport will still exist during the next 30 years. Oil is a flexible resource and easy to transport which keeps costs lower, especially when countries have reserves to last a long time (e.g. the USA has oil supplies to last 140 years – Figure 3). There are some problems with using oil, such as the emissions of CO_2 (Figure 2) which are contributing to climate change and particles that are causing serious air pollution in cities such as Beijing in China. Also, oil is a finite resource and will run out, therefore there is a possibility that the world should prepare now for a world without oil. However, the option of using renewables such as wind energy cannot replace oil as they only account for a tiny amount of UK energy consumption in 2016 – 4.6 mtoe compared to 68 mtoe. Renewables can lower pollution but do have their own environmental problems, such as turbine blades killing birds and spoiling scenery (Figure 5b). So, in the period up to 2030, option 1 is best as any sudden change would make it difficult for industries and people to adjust, and there must be further improvements to the alternatives.

Page 61

① ⓐ Sentences to include: 2, 4 and 6

ⓑ Sentence order: 6, 4 and 2

② ⓒ Another strength of chosen option: 7

ⓓ Weakness of chosen option: 3

ⓔ Strengths of other options: 1 and 5

③ Student's own answer

Page 62

Chosen option: 2 Use mostly wind energy
Using wind energy, alongside other renewables, will be the best option for the next 30 years because it is a non-polluting energy source. There are great concerns about damage to the natural environment, especially greenhouse gas emissions which cause climate change, and wind energy offers the chance to reduce emissions from power stations. For example, in the USA, 12.3 gigatonnes of greenhouse gas emissions could be avoided with investment in wind energy.
Wind energy produces very cheap electricity which can lower total energy costs for people or businesses; this allows people to afford other things to improve their lives or businesses to make more profit.
There are some problems with wind energy. These include the fact that it is still a developing technology and may not play a major part in energy production until 2050 in big energy consuming countries such as the USA. In 2014, 'renewables' only accounted for 7.5% of the world's total energy consumption (Fig. 1).
Oil is a very important energy resource at the moment, accounting for about a third of the world's energy consumption in 2014 because it can be used in a variety of ways – from cars to heating to industries. It may take some time to change away from this because oil-using technologies are well established. However, oil will run out (Fig. 2) and so change must happen at some point in the future.

uses geographical terminology

uses a sequence of paragraphs covering the structure of a justify answer

uses evidence from the resources to support the strengths and weaknesses identified

identifies strengths of the chosen option

identifies weaknesses of other option choices

links strengths and evidence to the question ✗

identifies one or more strengths of other options

identifies one or more weaknesses with the option choice

Page 63

① For example:

Paragraph 1: Oil reserves are available for the next 30 years (e.g. USA) (Figure 3). Oil only makes up about 30% of total world energy consumption (Figure 1).

Paragraph 2: Wind energy is good in windy locations, such as mountains (Figure 5b). Oil is a flexible resource that can be used anywhere (Figure 2).

Oil has established technologies (Figure 2). Need for investment and development of wind energy technologies (Figure 3).

Paragraph 3: Air pollution from oil (Figure 2), damage to the natural environment such as ANWR and fracking (Figure 3).

Paragraph 4: Option 1 – oil is finite (Figure 2). Option 2 – wind, solar and HEP energy only accounted for 4.6 mtoe of energy consumption in the UK in 2016 (Figure 4).

2 Some of the points you might make:

- There are still enough oil reserves for the next 30 years (e.g. USA) (Figure 3), but the development of renewable wind energy is necessary to help meet future energy needs as oil only makes up about 30% of world energy consumption (Figure 1).

- Wind energy is useful in exposed locations, such as mountains (Figure 5b) or offshore, but oil is a more flexible resource that can be used where these geographical conditions are not present (Figure 2).

- Oil has established technologies associated with it (Figure 2) and so businesses and people can continue to use this form of energy while there is the necessary investment and development of wind energy technologies (Figure 3).

- Pollution from oil will continue, especially CO_2 emissions (Figure 2), and there will also be an increase in damage to the natural environment as oil reserves are exploited in new landscapes with wildlife (e.g. ANWR) such as the use of fracking (Figure 3).

- Option 1 is not suitable because oil is finite and will run out soon (Figure 2), therefore we need to be developing other energy resources to replace oil.

- Option 2 is not suitable because wind, solar and HEP energy only accounted for 4.6 mtoe of energy consumption in the UK in 2016, compared to a total consumption of 192.8 mtoe (Figure 4), so it is too small on its own to meet energy needs over the next 30 years.

Notes

Notes

Notes

Notes